Working in English

Student's Book

WITHDRAWN

Leo Jones

CAMBRIDGE
UNIVERSITY PRESS

PUBLISHED BY THE PRESS SYNDICATE OF THE UNIVERSITY OF CAMBRIDGE
The Pitt Building, Trumpington Street, Cambridge, United Kingdom

CAMBRIDGE UNIVERSITY PRESS
The Edinburgh Building, Cambridge CB2 2RU, UK
40 West 20th Street, New York, NY 10011-4211, USA
10 Stamford Road, Oakleigh, VIC 3166, Australia
Ruiz de Alarcón 13, 28014 Madrid, Spain
Dock House, The Waterfront, Cape Town 8001, South Africa

http://www.cambridge.org

First published 2001

Printed in the United Kingdom at the University Press, Cambridge

Typeface Janson Monotype 11/14pt.   *System* QuarkXPress® [ODI]

A catalogue record for this book is available from the British Library

ISBN 0 521 77684 8   Student's Book
ISBN 0 521 77683 X   Teacher's Guide
ISBN 0 521 77685 6   Personal Study Book with Audio CD
ISBN 0 521 77682 1   Student's Book Audio Cassette Set
ISBN 0 521 77681 3   Student's Book Audio CD Set
ISBN 0 521 77679 1   Video [PAL]
ISBN 0 521 00851 4   Video [SECAM]
ISBN 0 521 00850 6   Video [NTSC]

Contents

Thanks and Acknowledgements

A big 'Thank You' to everyone who helped to create this course . . .

Will Capel commissioned the project, and kept a watchful eye on its progress.
Tony Garside edited the project expertly, sensitively and cheerfully.

Reviews and reports   Thanks to the business English teachers and experts who gave detailed feedback and helpful suggestions: Heather Bedell in Italy, Liz Bitterli in Switzerland, Trevor Bryant, Bernie Hayden and Sally Searby in the UK, Tracy Byrne and Mark Turner in Spain, Barbara Charlton, Gary Anderson, Geraint Marsh and Francis O'Hara in France, Eduardo Garbey Savigné in Cuba, Janaka Williams in Japan, Dan Schulte in Korea, Nigel McQuitty in Taiwan, Grazyna Siedlecka-Orzel in Poland, Debbie Goldblatt in the United States, and Richard Alexander.

Recordings   Thanks to everyone involved in the interviews and in the studio recordings: Isabel Boira Segarra (Mott Macdonald), Peter Callaghan, Will Capel, Charles Cotton (Virata), Tim Douglass, Tony Garside, Pete Kyle, Rich Le Page, Joost Meijerink (Flexifoil), Toby Nicol (easyJet), and the actors who contributed to the studio sessions.
Recording producer: Tim Douglass

Video   Thanks to Andrew Bampfield, Tyler Butterworth, Emma Ko, Pete Kyle and Pete Ravenscroft – and everyone at Marin in California and Waterford Wedgwood in Ireland.

Website   Thanks to Juliet Evans, Charles Shields and Roisin Vaughan.

Design   Thanks to Sam Dumiak in Cambridge, and Geoff Ager and Tony Archer at Oxford Designers & Illustrators
Picture research and photography: Hilary Fletcher
Permissions: Jayshree Ramsurun
Proofreader: Ruth Carim

The author and publishers are grateful to the authors, publishers and others who have given permission for the use of copyright material identified in the text. In the cases where it has not been possible to identify the source of material used, the publishers would welcome information from copyright owners.

For permission to include text:

Future Publishing Ltd. for p.28 'The e-mail revolution', from *MacFormat Magazine*.

For permission to include photographs, logos and other illustrative material:

Key: (*t*) = top; (*c*) = centre; (*b*) = bottom; (*l*) = left; (*r*) = right.

Will Capel for pp. 8, 10 (*c*), 78 (*b*); Tim Douglass for p. 74 (*br*); easyJet for p. 74 (*tl*); easyEverything for p. 74 (*tr*); Flexifoil for p. 78 (*t*); Robert Harding Picture Library for pp. 6 (*r*), 16 (*r*); Hotel del Coronado, Coronado, California for p. 69; Image Bank/Color Day for p. 6 (*l*), /Don Klumpp for p.24 (*r*), /Ghislain & Marie David de Lossy for p. 24 (*l*); International Business Channel (Europe) Ltd for p. 80; Leo Jones for p. 10 (*b*); www.lingodirect.com for p. 129; Pictor International for pp. 10 (*tl*), 52 (*l*); Powerstock Zefa for pp. 44, 46 (*l*), 52 (*tc, bc*), 66 (*tr*); The Stock Market/Jose L Pelaez, Inc. for p. 38 (*l*), /Jeff Zaruba for p. 66 (*bl*), /David Raymer for p. 66 (*br*), /Cameron for p. 72 (*l*); Tony Stone Images/Coneyl Jay for p. 12 (*r*), /Frank Herholdt for p. 19, /David Hanover for p. 50 (*r*), /Steven Peters for p. 56, /Sean Murphy for p. 72 (*r*); Superstock for pp. 52 (*r*), 66 (*tl, tc*), /Lisette Le Bon for p. 82; Telegraph Colour Library/V.C.L for pp. 10 (*tr*), 58, /Mel Yates for p. 16 (*l*), /Philippe Zamora for p. 18, /Robin Davies for p. 38 (*r*), /V.C.L/Nick Clements for p. 46 (*r*), /Stephen Simpson for p.50 (*l*), /V.C.L/ Spencer Rowell for p. 54, /Mike Malyszko for p. 66 (*bc*); Ultmost Corp for p. 144.

The following photographs were taken on commission for CUP by:
Trevor Clifford for pp. 12, 14, 40, 48, 62, 64, 70, 79.

For permission to include copyright cartoons:

CartoonStock for 7, 13, 17 (*b*), 23, 25 (*b*), 37, 57, 59, 65, 85.

Illustrators: Bob Wilson for p. 25 (*tl, tr*), Dave Bowyer for the map on p. 68; all other illustrations by Oxford Designers and Illustrators.

Introduction

Who is *Working in English* for?

If you are someone who needs to use English in your work – now or in the future – then *Working in English* is for you!

What are the components of *Working in English*?

The **Student's Book** contains seven Modules, each of 5 or 6 Units. Each Module is based on a different theme, and each Unit covers a different aspect of the theme. The Units are divided into sections with different exercises and activities. Accompanying this is an audio CD/cassette set containing all the listening activities.

The **Personal Study Book** (with audio CD) contains seven Modules. There are interviews, reading texts and exercises to supplement and follow up the work you do in the Student's Book, with transcripts, answers and a vocabulary glossary at the back of the book. (Your teacher will recommend particular exercises for homework to follow up each unit in the Student's Book.)

The **Video** contains eight documentary programmes. The first programme is an introduction and the other seven accompany each Module in the Student's Book. All the speakers are real people, not actors.

What does the Student's Book contain?

Speaking   Role plays and discussions give you a chance to practise using English and help you to become more confident in speaking English. In most of the speaking activities you'll be working in pairs or in groups. It's important to use English all the time when you're working with partners – because the only way to improve your spoken English is by *speaking* it!

The speech balloons give you useful phrases to help you to speak in a clear, polite and friendly way.

Files   Some role plays are in specially-numbered 'Files', where each person looks at different information. The Files are printed on separate pages (pages 118 to 144) so that you can't read each other's information and a natural conversation develops between you.

Listening   The recordings for *Working in English* include many different voices speaking at their natural speed. The tasks in the book help you to understand the main points the speakers make. (There are Transcripts of the recordings at the back of the book.)

Vocabulary   New vocabulary is introduced indirectly through the activities and exercises. When you come across a useful new word or expression in the book, why not highlight it? This will help you to remember the new words you meet.

Reading   There are several reading texts, with questions for discussion, and e-mails, letters and faxes for you to read and act upon.

Writing   Writing tasks help you to improve your writing skills.

Cross-cultural communication   Some units help you to deal more effectively with people from different countries and cultures.

Advice boxes   These contain tips and advice on business behaviour and using English in business situations.

Grammar Reference   Pages 86 to 101 explain the main 'problem areas' of English grammar with rules and examples.

Transcripts   There are Transcripts of the listening exercises on pages 102 to 117. Your teacher will advise you when to look at these.

Thank you for reading this introduction. Enjoy *Working in English*!

Leo Jones

1 Pleased to meet you!

Meeting people for the first time

1 👥 **In your country, when business people meet for the first time, what do they usually do? Put ticks or crosses in the boxes to show your answers:**

✔✔ = usually   ✔ = sometimes   ✗ = not usually   ✗✗ = never

- They exchange business cards.
- They shake hands.
- They bow to each other.
- They talk about a neutral subject (such as the weather) before getting down to business.
- They get down to business right away.
- One offers the other a cigarette.
- They have a drink together.
- They have a meal together.

2 🔊 **Listen to two conversations where people are meeting for the first time. Tick the questions you hear.**

How are you?	*How's it going?*
Did you have a good journey?	*How was your journey?*
Did you have any difficulty finding the office?	*Did you manage to find us all right?*
Is this your first visit to Paris?	*Have you been here before?*
Would you like something to eat?	*Have you had lunch?*

3 👥 **Work in pairs. What other questions can you think of for the situations above?**

⭐ You never get a second chance to make a good first impression.

B

1 Look at these phrases which you can use when meeting someone on business. **Highlight the phrases you want to remember.**

Host/Receptionist	Visitor
Good morning. Are you Mr Brown?	Good morning, yes, I'm Tony Brown.
	I have an appointment with Mrs Green.
Hello, Mr Brown, my name's Sam Allen. Pleased to meet you.	
Mrs Green will be back in a few minutes.	Nice to meet you, Sam. Do call me Tony.
Would you like to sit down?	
Can I take your coat?	
Can I get you something to drink?	Thank you. That's very kind of you.
Would you like some coffee or tea?	Coffee would be nice, please.
How do you like your coffee?	Black/white please, no sugar/two sugars.

2 👥 You are Kim Wilson. What can you say to Mr Jones in this conversation? Communicate the ideas in brackets. Write your exact words in the blanks, using some of the phrases above.

You: *Oh, good afternoon, are you Mr Jones?*
Mr Jones: Yes, good afternoon. I'm here to see Kim Wilson.

You: _____ (That's you!)
Mr Jones: It's nice to meet you too, Kim.

You: _____ (Welcome him, offer a seat.)
Mr Jones: Oh, yeah, thanks.

You: _____ (Offer him a drink.)
Mr Jones: Oh, yes, please, could I have some coffee?

You: _____ (White?)
Mr Jones: Oh, no, thanks, black, please, without sugar.

You: _____ (Does he want something to eat?)
Mr Jones: No, no thanks, I'm all right, I had lunch on the plane.

You: _____ (Ask about his journey.)
Mr Jones: Oh, you know, not too bad . . .

3 🔊 Listen to the recording and compare your ideas with the model version.

4 👥 Role-play meeting someone for the first time. Take turns to be the host and the visitor.

C

1 👥 Imagine that you are attending a conference and want to get to know some fellow-delegates. You'll be role-playing meeting them for the first time. One of you should look at **File 1** on page 118, the other at **File 31** on page 130. Follow the instructions there.

2 👥👥 After the role play, discuss these questions:
- How did you get better at meeting people for the first time?
- What would you do differently next time?
- How are real-life meetings different from the role play?

"First, as an ice breaker, how many of you have tattoos?"

www.CartoonStock.com

7

2 What do you do?

Finding out about work routines

Charles Cotton

Peter Callaghan

1 👥 **Look at the photos and discuss this question:**

● What kind of work do you think each person does?

2 🔊 👥 **Listen to Charles and Peter talking about their work. Fill the blanks in the summaries below.**

Charles Cotton is Chief _____ Officer of Virata, a software and semi-conductor company. The company's _____ Office is in California and employs _____ people in different locations around the world.

His job is satisfying because the company has been _____, and it's exciting to see the way they are helping to change the nature of communications in the _____.

Peter Callaghan is a 'company _____'. His job is to help unsuccessful companies to make a profit. He does this by encouraging the people in the company to _____ their attitudes and this leads to a change in the success of the company. But not every employee can do this. He has a saying: 'If you can't change the people, you have to _____ the people' – and employees who won't change, lose their _____.

3 🔊 👥 **Listen to Charles and Peter describing a typical day. Answer the questions by writing *C* for Charles or *P* for Peter next to each one.**

Which of them ...

.... starts work at 7 am?
.... starts work at 9 am?
.... doesn't switch on his computer when he first gets to the office?
.... receives up to 100 e-mails a day?

.... doesn't receive much mail?
.... has meetings with people outside the company, such as investors?
.... has meetings with project teams?
.... has two or three meetings a day?

4 👥👥 **Discuss these questions:**

● What are the differences between your own job (or a job you would expect to have) and their jobs?
● How would you feel if Peter was called in as 'company doctor' in your company?

B 1 👥 Match these questions to the numbered fields on the screen below.

a *What's your name?*

b *When do you work on Saturdays?*

c *If you're not in the office, who is the best person for me to talk to?*

d *What is your busiest time of day? When do you prefer not to receive phone calls?*

e *What is your phone number / e-mail address / fax number?*

f *What is your quietest time of day? When is the best time to phone you?*

g *What is the best way to get in touch with you quickly? By phone, e-mail or fax?*

h *What is the time difference between here and your country?*

i *What time do you start work in the morning? When do you finish work?*

j *What time do you usually go for lunch?*

k *What do you do? / What's your job?*

l *What's the name of your company?*

m *What's the postal address?*

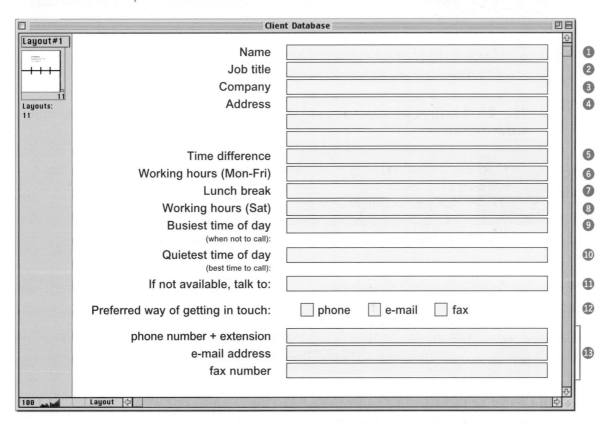

2 👥 Ask each other questions and complete the fields in the database with information about your partner. (Use your imagination and make up the information about yourself, if necessary.)

3 👥 Work with a different partner. Ask questions to find out about the person your partner was talking to in 2.

4 👥 One of you should look at File 2 on page 118, the other at File 32 on page 130. You'll be helping each other to fill in the missing information for two clients.

3 Around the world

Being sensitive to other people's customs, culture and behaviour

A **1** 👥 **You'll hear Charles Cotton and Isabel Boira Segarra talking about their experiences of working in California and Spain. Before you listen to the recordings, try to fill some of the blanks in the summaries below.**

2 🔊 👥 **Listen to the interviews and fill the blanks, using the words on the right.**

In technology companies in California, people work at least a ☐-hour day. They start before ☐ am and finish at ☐ or ☐ pm. They are in bed by ☐ pm. The idea of a '☐' day started in California, but now people are ☐ smartly again.

Even though Charles is Chief Executive Officer, everyone calls him by his ☐ name. The working environment is ☐ and there is not much hierarchy. Every ☐ the staff have an informal ☐ where they can ☐ each other on what's happening in different ☐.

10	12
7	7	8

first
dress-down
dressing up
areas
Friday
get-together
relaxed
update

There are many public holidays in Spain. Employess have to take their main holiday in a block in ☐. If there is a holiday on a ☐, people often take the Friday off, too. In ☐ many people take a whole week off.

In Isabel's experience, Spanish people have a ☐ attitude to time. There is often a lot of ☐ in offices. A Spanish office is more ☐ than an English office. She has to remember to keep her ☐ down in England.

noisy
November
relaxed
August
Friday
smoke
Thursday
voice

3 👥👥 **Discuss these questions:**

- Which of the points that Isabel and Charles made are also true about your country?
- When do co-workers use first names in your country?
- Would you call your boss by his/her first name?
- What kind of clothes do people wear for business in your country?
- What are the normal working hours in a factory and in an office in your country?
- How much do people socialize with each other after work?

4 **What advice can you give to Charles and Isabel if they visit your country?**

> People don't usually . . .   It's better to . . .

B **1** **There are many aspects of non-verbal behaviour that vary across cultures. This text focuses on two: the use of space and touching. Read the text and discuss these questions:**

- Do you agree with the text?
- What (other) similarities and differences are there between your culture and the ones mentioned in the text?
- What other aspects of non-verbal behaviour should business people be aware of?

The use of space

How close should you sit to someone when you are doing business? Of course, it will depend on where you are: in the office, restaurant or boardroom. And whether you are dealing with someone of the same or opposite sex, and standing or sitting.

However, you should always bear in mind that people will have a different 'space bubble' depending on their background. For example, people from the Mediterranean tend to sit or stand closer together than Northern Europeans or East Asians when doing business.

And if you are from a large 'space bubble' culture and meet someone from a small 'space bubble' culture, stepping back may be misunderstood. It may look like you don't like the person.

Touching

Business people touch when they shake hands, but the strength of the handshake can vary. In Germany it is firm, whereas in France it is light. As for other forms of physical contact, it is all right to pat someone on the shoulder or slap them on the back in the USA, but in the UK people sometimes don't like this sort of behaviour.

2 **Imagine that a new colleague from another country has come to work in your office. (Think of a workplace you know – or imagine a typical workplace in your country.) You're sitting together having coffee. How would you answer these questions?**

> What are the working hours?   Is it OK to call colleagues by their first name?
> What sort of clothes should I not wear? Is there a dress code in the office?
> When is lunchtime? How long do we have for lunch?

- What other questions might the new colleague ask you?
- What questions would you ask him or her to be friendly?

3 **One of you should look at** File 3 **on page 119, the other at** File 34 **on page 131. You'll be taking part in a role play.**

If you visit another country, don't expect everyone to behave in the same way that you do. Remember that foreign visitors to your country may find things strange and may not behave in the 'right' way – so be tolerant!

4 Could you please . . . ?

Offering to help • Making requests • Asking permission

A 1 Imagine that Anna and Ben, the people in the pictures, are colleagues of yours. What would you say to them? Decide which phrases you would say and tick the boxes.

	To Anna	To Ben	To neither
I'll see if I can make it work, if you like.			
I'll turn up the air-conditioning, if you like.			
Is there anything I can do?			
Leave it to me, I'm an expert.			
Shall I try to fix it for you?			
Shall I turn down the heating?			
Why don't you go outside for some fresh air?			
Why don't you take off some of your clothes?			
Would you like me to help you with that?			
Would you like me to open the window?			

2 **Look at the phrases below. Imagine that you didn't offer to help them.**

● What can Anna and Ben say to REQUEST your help – and how would you reply?

● What can Anna and Ben say if they want to ask your PERMISSION – and how would you reply?

offering to do something	Shall I . . .? Would you like me to . . .?
yes	Oh, yes, please. That's very kind of you.
no	No, don't worry. I can manage.
making a request	Could you please . . .? Please could you . . .?
yes	Yes, certainly. All right.
no	I'm afraid not because . . . I'm sorry, I can't because . . .
asking permission	Do you mind if I . . .? Would anyone mind if I . . .?
yes	Go ahead. No, of course not.
no	I'm afraid you can't do that because . . .

3 🔊 **Listen to the recording and practise saying the phrases.**

If you want to sound polite, say 'Please', 'Thank you' and 'You're welcome' a lot. If someone's not looking directly at you (and can't see your smiling face), it's best to be very polite – especially on the phone where they can only hear your voice.

B **1** 👥 **Take turns to play each role in this conversation.**

Before you begin the role play, you may find it helpful to go through it together deciding exactly what you're going to say. Then take part in the role play together.

Say hello.	
	Say hello. Ask if he/she has a problem.
There's a paper jam in the photocopier.	
	Offer to help.
Accept the offer.	
	Explain what you're doing as you lift the lid, take out the jammed paper and close the lid.
Thank him/her.	
	Ask if you can make a couple of copies first.
Agree.	
	Thank your colleague. Make two copies. Say you've finished.
Say you hope it doesn't go wrong again.	
	Wish your colleague good luck and say goodbye.
Say thanks and goodbye.	

2 🔊 **Listen to the recording and compare your ideas with the model version.**

3 👥 **One of you should look at File 4 on page 119, the other at File 35 on page 131. You'll have some mini-situations to role-play.**

MINE WORKS FLEXITIME TOO

www.CartoonStock.com

5 I'm sorry, could you say that again?

Dealing with communication difficulties

Ms Brown and Tom White

Mr Andrews and Lisa Wood

A

1 👥 What do you think is happening in the photos? How do the people feel, do you think?

2 🔊 👥 Listen to recordings of the two situations in the pictures. Note down why the situations are difficult. Listen again and decide what Tom White and Lisa Wood should say, and write it down.

> Ms Brown, the client, is asking Tom White for information about a product.
>
> It's difficult for Tom because . . . .
> Tom should say . . . .

> Lisa Wood is asking Mr Andrews, the supplier, when the goods will be shipped.
>
> It's difficult for Lisa because . . . .
> Lisa should say . . . .

3 🔊 👥 Listen to what Tom and Lisa actually said, and write it down. Who coped better with the difficult situation? What do you think will happen next?

> Tom: ....
> Lisa: ....

(B) 1 👥 Various things may make it difficult to understand people talking English. Which of the following do you find difficult? Which is the worst problem for you?

- a native speaker talking fast
- a native or non-native speaker with a strange accent
- a non-native speaker who makes mistakes in English
- background noise (traffic, machinery, etc.)
- other people talking in the background
- (on the phone) not being able to see the other person's face, body language and gestures

2 🔊 👥 Listen to SEVEN clips of people making requests and asking for information. Choose the correct answer for each. Compare your answers and then listen again.

1 Ms A wants to know . . .
    the retail price   the wholesale price   neither of these   both of these

2 Mr B's extension number is . . .
    4458   5844   8544

3 Ms C's assistant is called . . .
    Henry Duval   Henri Duvalier   Henry Duvalier   Henri Duval

4 How many boxes does Mr D require altogether?
    30   45   60   75

5 The contract must be ready for Ms E by the . . .
    15th of this month   14th of next month   4th of next month

6 What is the name of Mr F's hotel?
    King   King's   Kingsway   Kingswood   Seafront

7 What is the product number that Ms G mentions?
    141220   121420   121402   141202

3 In real life you can't rewind a recording to hear people again. Which of these phrases would you use to respond to the people in each situation?

> I'm sorry, could you say that again, please?
>
> Did you say . . . or . . . ?
>
> Do you mean . . . ?
>
> How do you spell that?
>
> Could you say those figures again more slowly, please?
>
> Can I just check that I've noted that down correctly?
>
> Could you write that down for me, please?

4 🔊 👥 Listen to the model responses. Then practise saying the phrases.

5 👥 One of you should look at File 6 on page 120, the other at File 37 on page 132. You'll each have some information to give to the other, which you'll have to repeat or spell aloud.

6 Hello, how may I help you?

Answering the phone • Making a good impression on the phone

A 1 Read the list of tips and decide which are DOs and which are DON'TS.

When you answer the phone in the office . . .

pick it up after the first ring

pick it up after three or more rings

immediately ask who is calling and what they want

say your own name

say your company name and/or department

just say 'Hello?'

have a pencil and paper ready so that you can take notes

try to sound friendly and helpful

speak quickly so that the call is soon over

speak clearly and slowly

smile

2 Listen to two people trying to call Celia Sharpe. Discuss why the first caller gets a bad impression and why the second caller gets a better impression.

The first caller gets a bad impression because the person who answered didn't . . .

The second caller gets a good impression because the person who answered remembered to . . .

Answer the phone in a friendly, confident voice – the other person can't see you, so their impression of you depends on the way you sound.

B 1 🔊 Listen to Peter Blake and Mandy Green answering the phone. Decide if they sound polite and helpful when they say the phrases below. Put a tick in the box when they sound polite and helpful – and a cross when they don't.

Peter Blake		Mandy Green
✔	Good morning. How may I help you?	☐
☐	Good morning. Compass International.	☐
☐	This is . . . speaking.	☐
☐	I'm sorry, (but) she's not here just now.	☐
☐	Is there anything I can do to help?	☐
☐	Can I give her a message?	☐

2 Practise saying the same phrases yourself in a polite and helpful voice.

C 1 🔊 Listen to these useful phrases which you can use on the phone. Practise saying them.

I'd like to speak to . . ., please.
Could I speak to . . ., please?

please wait	Could you hold the line a moment, please? Sorry to keep you waiting.
not available	I'm afraid he's not available at the moment. He's not at his desk at the moment. I'm afraid she's not here at the moment. She won't be back till 2:30. Can I ask her to call you when she's free?
goodbye	Thank you for calling. Goodbye.

2 👥 One of you should look at File 7 on page 120, the other at File 38 on page 132. You'll each have some phone calls to make.
Don't face each other during your calls. Use only your voices to communicate – not gestures and eye contact.

3 👥 + 👥 Discuss these questions:
• What improvements did you make in your phone-answering skills?
• What would you do differently next time?
• How are real-life phone calls different from the role play?

"I'm phoning to let you know I've faxed you to say I've sent an email asking you to call me."

7 Hold on, I just need to make a note

Understanding numbers and details • Making notes • Checking your notes

A **1** Read this advice on making notes. Fill the blanks with suitable words.

IT'S EASIER to remember information later if you make _____ during a phone call.

When you receive information over the phone, make sure you understand it and note it down accurately. This is particularly important when noting down names, addresses, _____, dates and _____, and prices.

If you don't understand what someone has said, ask them to say it again more _____.

If you don't know how to spell a name, ask the other person to spell it out for you.

At the end of the call, read your _____ back to the other person to make sure you've got all the information right.

2 Compare your answers. Can you add any advice?

3 + Decide which of these are hardest to understand over the phone in English:

first names • family names • place names • addresses • postcodes/zip codes
e-mail addresses • phone or fax numbers • dates • times • percentages • prices

What other kinds of information are hard to understand?

B **1** Listen to two phone calls and note down the information missing from these notes.

Message from MADAME PINEAU
Order _____ is delayed:
Now leaving Paris Fri am
Arriving here _____ pm
Any questions: call her mobile
0789 983 _____

Mr Jeremy Lee
arriving Springfield _____ on May 2
Flight CX _____
Book non-smoking room _____ Hotel*
4 nights (to _____)
confirm by e-mail: jlee@ _____
*or Marriott

2 Compare your notes. Listen again and check your answers.

1  Listen to these phrases and practise saying them.

> *I'm sorry, could you say that again, please?*
> *Could you say that again more slowly, please?*
> *I'm sorry, I didn't quite catch what you said.*
> *I'm sorry, could you spell that for me, please?*
> *I'm sorry, did you say 14 or 40?*
> *Could I just check that I've noted the details down correctly?*

2 Before you begin the role play in 3, note down your name, phone number, company name and the time when you want to be called back. (Invent these details or use your own.)

3 Take turns to play each role in this phone conversation.
You may find it helpful to go through it together deciding exactly what you're going to say, before you actually begin the role play.

Answer the phone. Say who you are.

| | Say who you are. Ask to speak to Mrs Watson. |

| Say she's not available. Offer to take a message. | |

| | Ask when she's available. |

| Not till Monday. Offer to take a message. | |

| | Say when you'd like her to call you back. |

| Ask for the caller's number and extension. | |

| | Give your number and extension. |

| Ask the caller to spell his/her name. | |

| | Spell your name and company name. |

| Check that you have all the information down correctly. | |

| | Listen carefully, correct any mistakes, say goodbye. |

D **1** One of you should look at File 9 on page 121, the other at File 40 on page 133. You'll each have some information to give to the other in phone calls.
Don't face each other – rely on your voices to communicate. The role play is in FOUR parts.

2 + Discuss these questions:
- As the caller, how did you feel when you had to keep repeating things and spelling things?
- What extra difficulties will there be in real life, which didn't happen in the role play?
- What is the most useful thing you've learnt in this lesson?

8 # Is everything clear?

Taking long messages • Leaving messages

A **1** 🔊 👥 **Listen to the recording and then look at these versions of the same message. Each contains one mistake. Find the mistakes and then decide:**

- Which version is best? Why?
- What is good and bad about each?

> Emma Harris called
> Meeting on Mon postponed,
> reschedule for Tues am if poss.
> Best time: 11 am
> Book meeting room for 12 people
> + drinks & sandwiches.
> Meeting must end before 2 am.

> Emily Harris says the meeting on Monday is postponed.
> Is it possible to change this to Tuesday morning? Best starting time would be 11 am.
> Please book the Meeting Room for 11 people. Also arrange drinks and sandwiches.
> She says the meeting must end before 2 pm.

> E Harris called
> Meeting now Tues @ 11 — OK?
> Book room (12) + snack
> Must start before 2 pm

 However good your handwriting, it's usually best to rewrite a message to make it clear for someone else.

2 👥 **Using abbreviations can save time. (But don't use abbreviations if the meaning isn't clear to the reader.) Do you know (or can you guess) what these abbreviations mean?**

Feb Fri Sq Rd Ave if poss info asap no. OR # FYI BTW incl PTO Re:

(Answers in **File 45**)

B 👥 **Convert these sentences into notes.**

1 You can phone me any time but I won't be here after noon tomorrow.
2 I'd like you to send me a price list. If you can e-mail this, that would be fine.
3 Could you get someone to pick me up at the station? My train gets in at half past nine.
4 Can you book a hotel room for me from Sunday to Wednesday, if possible at the Grand?
5 For your information, the price of your hotel room includes breakfast.
6 Can you fax me a copy of the contract as soon as you can, please?
7 Could you please also send me any information you have on the meeting we had in February?
8 My telephone number is 555 8899, and the extension number is 990.

> Phone before 12 tomorrow.

C **1** 🔊 👥 Listen to a phone call and complete the notes on the left. Then compare your notes with a partner.

2 🔊 👥 Listen to a voice-mail message and complete the notes on the right. Then compare your notes with a partner.

MESSAGE FOR BARBARA BLACK
FROM MAX FISCHER
Re: Visit to _____ tomorrow —
changes to schedule
Pick up from hotel @ _____
1st appointment: _____
2nd appointment _____
(bring _____)
Rest of morning: _____

LUNCH with Herr Müller +
_____

P.M. Visit _____ + _____
Taxi to airport at _____

Any problems call Max on his cell
phone (_____)

MESSAGE FOR MAX FISCHER
FROM BARBARA BLACK

Got message about _____
Problem: _____
— now _____
Rearrange 1st + 2nd appointments
_____
— before or after _____

Return flight _____ , so _____
Call her on _____
1 to confirm _____
2 to confirm _____

Checklist: messages

☐ Is the message LEGIBLE? Will the other person be able to read it?

☐ Will someone else understand the message without having to ask you any questions?

☐ Does the message include ALL the relevant info?

☐ Are the details CORRECT – especially times, dates, names, addresses and numbers?

D **1** 🔊 Listen to these phrases which you can use when leaving a message. Practise saying them.

> Can I leave a message for . . . ?
> Could you give her this message, please?
> Is everything clear?
> Have you got that?
> Do you want me to repeat anything?

2 👥 One of you should look at File 10 on page 121, the other at File 41 on page 133. You'll each have a phone message to give to the other.

3 👥 When you've finished, look at the Checklist above. Can you answer *Yes* to the questions?

9 I'm calling because . . .

Preparing to make a phone call • Making different kinds of calls

A

1 🔊 👥 **Listen to Alan making a phone call to Sarah Bryant. Which of the things in this Checklist did Alan probably NOT do before he picked up the phone to call her?**

> **Checklist: before making a phone call**
>
> ☐ Do you have the relevant file and documents ready (on screen or on your desk)?
>
> ☐ What do you know about the person you're calling? How well does he or she know you?
>
> ☐ Have you noted down the questions you want to get answers to?
>
> ☐ Have you noted down the information you want to give?
>
> ☐ Are you calling at a convenient time? What time of day (or night) is it there?
>
> ☐ Do you have a notepad and pencil ready so that you can take notes?

2 👥 **Here's some advice on making business phone calls. Match the advice on the left to the reasons on the right.**

1 Make sure the other person knows who you are and why you're calling . . .

2 Ask the other person to repeat information you didn't catch . . .

3 Confirm that you've understood each point . . .

4 Double-check that you've noted down the other person's details correctly . . .

5 Offer to call back if you need time to check on information . . .

6 Offer to send detailed information by fax or e-mail . . .

7 Say if you can't answer a question . . .

8 Say when you don't understand . . .

a because dictating information over the phone is difficult and time-consuming.

b because if he or she says it more slowly, you may understand it the next time.

c because it's difficult to clear up misunderstandings later.

d because someone else in the office may know the answer.

e because the other person can't see you nodding.

f because the other person doesn't want to be put on hold for too long.

g because you must have this information exactly right.

h because he or she won't have to waste time trying to work this out.

3 👥 **Now match these sentences with the advice and reasons above.**

> *Can I just check that I've noted everything down correctly?*
>
> *Could you just hold the line a moment, please? I'll need to ask my colleague.*
>
> *I could e-mail that information to you or send you a fax.*
>
> *I'm not quite sure about that. Could I call you back in a few minutes, please?*
>
> *I'm sorry, I don't quite understand what you mean.*
>
> *Hello, my name's . . . The reason I'm calling you is that . . .*
>
> *Yes, I see. / Yes, I understand.*
>
> *I'm sorry, could you say that again more slowly, please?*

4 🔊 **Listen to the phrases and practise saying them.**

B 1 🔊 Listen to clips from two more phone calls.
Put a cross in the boxes to show which advice in the Checklist the woman ignored in conversation 1.
Tick the boxes to show which advice the man followed in conversation 2.

Checklist: while making a phone call	1	2
Tell the other person who you are and why you're calling.	☐	☐
Speak clearly and not too fast.	☐	☐
Speak in a polite and friendly tone of voice.	☐	☐
Make notes on the important information.	☐	☐
Ask the person to repeat anything you aren't sure about.	☐	☐
Double-check your notes to make sure they're correct.	☐	☐
Finish the call in a positive, friendly way.	☐	

2 This activity is in THREE parts so that everyone can try different roles. During each call one of you makes the call, one of you receives the call and one is the 'Observer'. The Observer's role is to listen and give feedback using the Checklist above.

👥👥👥 Work in groups of three. Student A should look at File 11 on page 122, Student B at File 42 on page 134 and Student C at File 63 on page 142.

3 👥👥👥 + 👥👥👥 Discuss these questions:
- What extra difficulties will there be in real life, which didn't happen in the role play?
- What did you find most difficult in the role plays?
- How useful was the feedback you got from the Observer?

"Almost finished."

I'm terribly sorry

Dealing with problems on the phone

A 1 🔊 👥 **Jack is answering the phone. Listen to the beginning of the call. Which of the following should he say next?**

> Are you quite sure you did tell me?
>
> Could you tell me your new e-mail address?
>
> I'm sorry, could you say that again? It's a very bad connection/line.
>
> I'm terribly sorry about that.

🔊 **Listen to the continuation of the call. Did Jack say what you expected him to say?**

2 🔊 👥 **Jenny is making a phone call. Listen to the beginning of the call. Which of the following should she say next?**

> Do you mind if I call you back in a minute? My computer has crashed again.
>
> I tried calling you several times but I couldn't get through.
>
> I tried calling you this morning but the line was busy all the time.
>
> I'm sorry, I couldn't call you because I was sick.

🔊 **Listen to the continuation of the call. Did Jenny say what you expected her to say?**

3 👥👥 **Discuss these questions:**

- When do people need to apologize in business?
- Do you try to avoid saying sorry to people, or do you admit your mistakes?
- What was one of the most difficult apologies you've had to make?

B 1 🔊 👥 **Listen to these phrases and practise saying them.**

breaking bad news

> Hello, Mr Page, I'm sorry to trouble you but . . .
>
> I'm afraid I have some rather bad news.
>
> I'm very sorry about this but . . .

reacting to bad news

> Yes, what seems to be the problem?
>
> Oh, dear, what's happened?.

apologizing

> I'm really very sorry about this.
>
> I'd like to apologize for this.
>
> I'll certainly make sure it doesn't happen again.

reacting to an apology

> Don't worry, It doesn't really matter.
>
> It's OK really. I hope it won't happen again.
>
> That's all right.

2  Take turns to play each role in this phone conversation.

You may find it helpful to go through it together deciding exactly what you're going to say, before you actually begin the role play.

Answer the phone. Say you are Tom Davis.

Say who you are. Ask Mr Davis how he is.

Say that you're fine.

Say you have some bad news for him.

Ask what the problem is.

Explain the problem: A serious bug has been found in the software he is expecting from you this week.

Ask when the software will be ready.

Say you can't promise a new date. It depends on how quickly your engineers can sort it out.

Say you're disappointed. But it's good that the bug was discovered before you got the software.

Promise to tell him when you know a firm date for shipment. Apologize again.

Accept the apology and end the call.

3 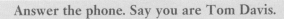 Work in groups of four. Two of you should look at File 16 on page 124, the others at File 47 on page 136. You'll take part in TWO prepared role plays. First, you'll prepare for each phone call with your partner and then join a different person for the role play.

4 Discuss these questions:
- What did you find most difficult in the role plays?
- What would you do differently if you could do the role plays again?
- What extra difficulties will there be in real life, which didn't happen in the role play?

"New York are out for breakfast, Munich are having a coffee break and Tokyo are at lunch."

11 Layout and content

Good layout and style in letters and faxes

A 1 👥 **Read this letter through carefully. Match these labels to the parts of the letter.**

addressee • date • ending • greeting • introduction • letterhead • main body of the letter
name and job title of sender • signature • subject

1

Wonderful Letters plc

1000 Utopia Boulevard
Monte Cristo
FR-900 Fredonia
phone: 09 777 7777   fax: 09 777 7000   http://www.wonderful-letters.com

2

Reader
Page 26
Working in English

3

today's date

4

Dear Reader,

5

Writing a good letter, fax or e-mail

6

Thank you for your enquiry about our services. You asked us for some advice on improving your correspondence.

Here are 7 important rules:

1. Plan ahead. Decide what you want to say before you start writing. Make notes.

2. Look professional. A clean, logical format gives the best impression. A crowded or over-designed page will distract from your messsage. Leave a line space between each paragraph.

3. Keep it simple. Don't use complicated langage. Keep your sentences short – one idea in each. Any sentence longer than two typed lines is probably too long. Shorter sentences are easier to read.

7

4. Put yourself in your reader's place. Try to imagine how you would respond to the same letter. Have you given the right impression?

5. Be friendly. Your correspondence should read like a conversation with the reader. Use your reader's name if you know it: 'Dear Ms Green,'. You want her to know you wrote the letter just for her. Use 'I', 'we' and 'you'.

6. Reply in the same style. If someone writes a friendly letter to you using contractions like 'don't' and 'can't', use the same style in your reply.

7. Re-read the letter before sending it. Does it give the right impression? Check for speling mistakes and punctuation errors. Make sure that all the information you give is accurate.

I hope some of this helps you to write better letters. If you have any questions, please let me know.

8

Yours sincerely,

9

Leo Jones

PS I made three spelling mistakes in this letter ! Did you spot them ?

10

Leo Jones, Correspondence Manager
e-mail leojones@wonderful-letters.com

---

2 👥👥 **What were the spelling mistakes? What was the most valuable piece of advice?**

B 1 👥 Look at this fax and the reply to it. Which of the rules in A1 has the writer of the reply not followed?

10 May

Please let me know when to expect
shipment of our order no. 4567.
Shipment was promised for 2 May
but there is no sign of the
consignment.
Yours sincerely,
David Brown

Dear Sir,

Thanks for your letter.

According to our shiping department the goods left here at 14.30 on 1 May and were due to arrive on 3 May at the latest so after receiving your letter I tried to contact the manager of the shipping company but he isn't answering the phone. I'll keep trying and get in touch when I have some news.

I am sure you'll get the goods soon, and I hope you understand it's not our fault. But I'm very sorry it's happened anyway.

Yours faithfully

Alex Clark

PS I forgot to mention that we have not had any problems with the shipping company before.

2 👥 Draft a better reply to Mr Brown's fax. Try to follow the advice suggested opposite.

3 👥 + 👥 Exchange faxes with another pair. Imagine that you are Mr Brown and the shipment has just arrived. Write a reply to the other pair's fax.

Useful phrases

Thank you for your recent letter/fax (your ref. 5589).
Thank you for your enquiry about our products.

I am writing to confirm that...   I am writing to enquire whether...

We are pleased to inform you that...   I am happy to tell you that...
We regret to inform you that...   I am sorry to have to tell you that...
I will let you know as soon as I have any further news.
Please accept our apologies for the delay.

Looking forward to hearing from you.
I am looking forward to meeting you on May 1st.

If you have any further questions, please call me or e-mail me.
If I can help you in any way, please e-mail me at the address below.

(GB) Yours sincerely,   (USA) Sincerely,

12 You've got mail

Sending and receiving e-mail messages

A **1** **Read this text and fill the blanks with words from this list. Then discuss the questions below.**

letter • once • record • send • understand • language

The e-mail revolution

Many people find that their e-mail program is as indispensable as their Web browser. While the Web is all about information, e-mail is all about communication. Just as the phone has almost completely replaced the _____ as a means of staying in touch with friends and family, so e-mail is threatening to do the same to business correspondence – or even to the phone.

The biggest revolution is in international communications. Most people struggling with a second language find it much easier to _____ a written e-mail than speech, with all its imperfections, inflections and regional accents. Even when you're both talking the same _____, it can be much easier to express a complex idea – or a controversial point! – in carefully-composed words rather than in a live conversation. Most of all, you can _____ an e-mail at any time of day, without having to allow for different global time zones.

What's more, telephone conversations are transitory. Unless you take notes (or record them), there's no permanent _____ of what was said, by whom and when. But you can keep, archive, and even search your e-mail correspondence.

You can forward it to others, too, either singly or as a group. No matter how many people you send an e-mail to, you only have to send it _____ – the Internet looks after the rest.

- How many advantages of e-mail are mentioned? Highlight them all.
- If, as the text says, e-mail is so wonderful, why do business people still send letters and faxes?
- Why do they still use the phone?
- How many disadvantages of e-mails can you think of?
- How many e-mails do you send and receive on a typical day?

2 🔊 👥 **Listen to a voice-mail message. Make notes on the main points.**

3 **Write the same message as an e-mail.**

4 👥 + 👥 **Compare your e-mails. Then discuss these questions:**
- What did you find difficult about writing the e-mail?
- How long did it take you to write it?
- Why do you think Sam decided to phone Fritz rather than send an e-mail?

Checklist: writing e-mails

☐ Keep your message short – people don't like long e-mails.

☐ Don't use abbreviations unless you're quite sure your reader will understand them.

☐ Only use capital letters for special emphasis. CAPITALS look as if you're SHOUTING!!

☐ Don't use <u>underlining</u> – underlining looks like a hyperlink to a website.

☐ For clarity, put a complete line space between each paragraph.

☐ Make sure your spelling and grammar are reasonably correct.

☐ Never send an e-mail without checking it through carefully. If you receive an e-mail containing information that isn't clear to you, reply to it quickly and ask for clarification.

☐ Make sure you have attached any attachments you want to send.

☐ Make sure you're sending it to the right person!

B 1 👥 Write replies to these e-mails, using the information given on the right. Some of the phrases in the box below may be helpful.

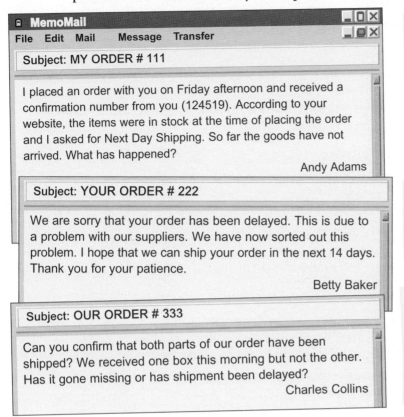

MemoMail ‗ ☐ ☒

File   Edit   Mail   Message   Transfer

Subject: MY ORDER # 111

I placed an order with you on Friday afternoon and received a confirmation number from you (124519). According to your website, the items were in stock at the time of placing the order and I asked for Next Day Shipping. So far the goods have not arrived. What has happened?

Andy Adams

Subject: YOUR ORDER # 222

We are sorry that your order has been delayed. This is due to a problem with our suppliers. We have now sorted out this problem. I hope that we can ship your order in the next 14 days. Thank you for your patience.

Betty Baker

Subject: OUR ORDER # 333

Can you confirm that both parts of our order have been shipped? We received one box this morning but not the other. Has it gone missing or has shipment been delayed?

Charles Collins

Next Day Shipping only for orders placed before noon. Orders placed after noon Fri not shipped until Mon. Goods will arrive before 5 pm on Tues – let me know if they don't.

Cancel order. Customer wanted goods this week – can't wait longer.

Sorry. Both boxes shipped together. What is no. on box that did arrive?
If missing box doesn't arrive/is damaged, we will replace it free of charge.

2 👥 + 👥 Show your replies to another pair and read theirs. Have they followed the advice in the Checklist on page 28?

Useful phrases	
opening	Thank you for your enquiry/e-mail. Thank you for ordering from us. In reply to your request I can confirm that . . .
reason for writing	I'm sorry I wasn't available to take your call yesterday. I tried to phone you this morning but you were out of the office. I'm sorry for the delay in replying to your e-mail but I needed to check some information with our shipping department. I can now confirm that your order has been shipped by air freight. It should reach you in two days. Thank you for your e-mail. There is one point I don't quite understand. Can you please confirm that the catalogue number of the item you require is 33/444-A? I am sorry to inform you that we have to cancel this order.
request for action	Could you please call me later today? Please confirm that these arrangements are OK.
ending	Regards, (USA) Sincerely, (USA) Best,	Yours truly, (GB) Yours sincerely, (GB) Best wishes,

13 Get it right!

Checking your spelling • Correcting your punctuation

Spelling mistakes give a bad impression. If you don't seem to care about spelling mistakes, it may look as if you don't care about your reader.

Always check correspondence before you send it. Use a spell-checker if possible. Check your correspondence for keyboard errors (like 'Amercian', 'Britihs' or 'hte').

A

1 **Look at this letter and find the spelling mistakes in it. There are 13 altogether.**

2 **Write a short reply to the letter. Then check your reply for spelling mistakes.**

> Dear Mr Rodriguez,
>
> Thank you for sending us your catlogue and box of sampels.
>
> I would like to place a trial order for the folowing items:
>
> 100 Roller Coaster 20-oz glasses @ 63 cents each
>
> 100 Spinning Wheel 10-oz glasses @ 54 cents each
>
> Please confirm that you have recieved this order and that you will be able to shipp the goods too reach us by November 5, in time for our Chrismas seeson.
>
> I understand that shiping charges will ammount to 15% of the total order.
>
> I hope that, if sails of these items are good, we will be able to plaice further larger orders next year.
>
> Yours sincerly,

3 **Find the spelling mistakes in these commonly misspelt words. Tick the correct words and change the incorrect ones.**

adress   advertize   believe   cheif   comercial   convenient   corespondance
eficient   faithfuly   foriegn   infomation   pateince   piece   receive   reciept
sincerly   supervize   thier

> There should be two Rs in 'correspondence'.
>
> 'Correspondence' ends in Ence not Ance.
>
> This word looks OK to me – what do you think is wrong with it?

If you have an English spell-checker, use it. But don't rely on it to spot every mistake.

A spell-checker can't detect that 'Thanks you four you're patients' should be 'Thank you for your patience'! It can only detect mistakes like these: speling, grammer, misteak.

E-mails are quicker to write than letters because most business people are tolerant of mistakes. They read their e-mails quickly and may not notice a few spelling mistakes or minor errors in grammar.

But readers WILL notice if you make A LOT OF mistakes – and may not understand!

The purpose of punctuation is to make your meaning clear. Most punctuation is similar in different languages, but be careful about the small differences between your own language and English.

B **1** 👥 **Add punctuation to this fax and correct the keyboard errors.**

> Dear Mr Black
>
> I d like to order the follwing
>
> 40 fourty pairs of Arctic brand gloves @ €59 fifty-nine euros per pair
>
> Please confrim by fax e-mail that you have these itmes in stock
>
> If there are any problems please phone me on my direct line 44 1223 325844 or if you perfer you can e-mail me smurphy@criterionstores com
>
> Looking froward to hearing form you
>
> Yours sincerely
>
> Susan Murphy Mrs
>
> Chief Buyer

2 👥 **Match the following words in blue to the punctuation marks in red:**

.   ?   !   ,   :   –   •   /   "   "   (   )   '

bullet   colon   comma   dash   exclamation mark   quotation marks / quotes
question mark   slash / stroke   apostrophe   ⒼⒷ brackets / ⓊⓈⒶ parentheses
ⒼⒷ full stop / ⓊⓈⒶ period / dot (in e-mails and URLs) / point (for decimals and money)

3 👥 **Look at this very enthusiastic letter! Rewrite the letter, changing the punctuation to make the letter seem more formal and tasteful.**

> **Dear Mr Black!**
> **GREAT News for YOU!!**
> To commemorate the relaunch of our "TipTop" products we are making a **SPECIAL OFFER** for all our <u>regular</u> customers!
> The <u>whole</u> range is now available **AT A SPECIAL PRICE!!!**
> Yes, Mr Black, you can now order <u>any</u> item from the TipTop range at 25 per cent (Yes, that's right – **TWENTY-FIVE PER CENT**) off the regular price.
> **BUT** this offer is only available until November 30th.
> So, I urge you to check your inventory <u>now</u>. It could pay you to order <u>now</u> – rather than wait until next month.
> Looking forward to hearing from you!
> (Remember this **SPECIAL** offer expires on **November 30**.)

4 👥 + 👥 **Compare your answers. Then discuss these questions:**
- Are you good at spelling and punctuation in your language? Are you a good speller in English?
- What kinds of spelling mistakes do you make most in English:
  keyboard errors • careless mistakes • wrongly guessing the spelling
- Can you think of some ways of improving your spelling in English?

14 Keep it simple and make it clear

Writing simple sentences • Writing short reports on meetings and phone calls

A **1** Read this paragraph and decide which of the headings goes best with it.

Short sentences are easier to write – and to understand.
Long sentences will impress your reader.

> One of the main disadvantages of a long, complex sentence, which may still be found in some business correspondence despite the progress that has been made in recent years towards simplifying business writing styles in the English-speaking world, is that the reader is likely to find it more difficult to understand than a series of shorter sentences, which in turn may lead to frustration and misunderstanding, particularly if the reader is a busy person who has more important things to do. You want to communicate your message to the reader, not impress him or her with your command of English.

2 Look at these long, complicated sentences. Rewrite them using TWO simpler sentences in each case.

1
> In spite of our having had difficulties with our original suppliers it has been fortunately possible for us to find an alternative supplier and consequently we are pleased to inform you that your order will be shipped on Monday.

We had difficulties with our original suppliers but we have found an alternative supplier. I am pleased to inform you that we will ship your order on Monday.

2
> Although we discussed the advantages and disadvantages of bringing forward our delivery date, it was agreed that this might result in lower standards of quality.

We discussed bringing . . . . However, we agreed . . .

3
> As a consequence of Mr Brown's complaint about the inadequate quality of the goods I promised to investigate the matter and told him that I would telephone him on Monday to give him my report on the investigation.

Mr Brown complained . . . . call him on Monday.

4
> A possible solution to the problem might be found by having a meeting which is attended by the sales staff and the production manager.

3 + Compare your sentences. Then look at the advice on writing paragraphs.

Checklist: writing paragraphs

- [ ] Start a new paragraph for each new idea. Short paragraphs are easier to read.
- [ ] Leave a line space between each paragraph. If you do, there's no need to indent the first line.
- [ ] Short sentences are easier to understand – and to write – than long, complicated ones.
- [ ] Don't use a passive verb (the goods were shipped) if you can use an active verb (we shipped the goods) – active verbs are more personal.
- [ ] Use bullets (•) or numbers to show separate points.
- [ ] Use a different style for emphasis. The most common styles are:
  <u>underlining</u> *italics* **bold print** **coloured print** CAPITAL LETTERS SMALL CAPS
  – but don't overdo this: more than two styles in a report or letter may look silly.

1 **Listen to a phone call and look at this report on it. Fill the blanks in the report.**

J44 Prototype Faults

Mr Chang of Chang Products is concerned about the _____
the J44 prototype. I told him that we are redesigning the faulty
_____ and that a new prototype will be ready in a few days. He
would like his engineer to check the components before they go into
_____ I agreed this would be a good idea.

He is willing to send his engineer here to _____ prototype at
our expense. Alternatively, Mr Simpson could take the prototype with
him to Korea if it is ready by _____ n he leaves. The
first option would cost us more, but the second option depends on the
prototype being ready in time for Mr Simpson to take.

Mr Chang is due here himself on _____ he prototype is not likely
to be ready by then and Mr Chang says he is not _____
to inspect it himself.

2 Look at the notes below about your meeting with Mr Chang today. Your boss needs a
report on the meeting. Write a report, following the points in the Checklist on the right.

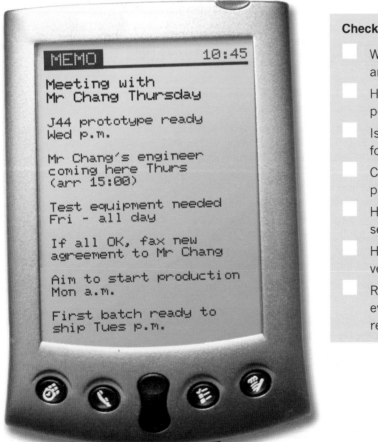

Checklist: report writing

- [ ] What information is essential, and what can be omitted?
- [ ] Have I covered all the main points?
- [ ] Is it clearly laid out and easy to follow?
- [ ] Can I get everything onto half a page?
- [ ] Have I used short, simple sentences?
- [ ] Have I used too many passive verbs?
- [ ] Re-read the report: will everything be clear to the reader(s)?

3 **Look at each other's reports.**

Is everything clear to you? Has your partner followed the advice in the Checklist? What
improvements can you suggest?

In reply to your . . .

Replying to letters, faxes and e-mails

A 1 Look at this e-mail and the first draft of the reply to it. There are EIGHT mistakes of different kinds which need to be corrected in the reply before it is sent – can you find them all?

Dear Ms Collins,

Thank you for sending us your catalogue. Could you please give me more information about your V44 and V55 systems?

1 Can you advise me which of them is more suitable for integration with a SuperFast P12?

2 We are planning to upgrade to SuperFast P2000 next year. Which of your systems integrates best with that?

3 What discounts do you offer for a large order? We would be thinking in terms of ordering four initially, and if they are satisfactory, a further twelve.

Best regards,

James Martinez

Dear Mr James,

Thank you for your e-mail and for your interest in our products.

I can assure you that both the V44 and V55 systems work perfectly with all models in the current SuperFast range, including the P12. I have a V44 working with a P12 myself, and have had no problems with it at all. The SuperFast P2000 is something of an unknown quantity at the moment. The manufacturers haven't released the specification yet. Our best guess is that we will need to modify the V44 and V55 to make them compatable. However, if this is necessery within one year of your purchase, we will make the modification free of charge.

The main difference between the V44 and V55 is that the V55 is slightly more expensive but much faster. I suggest that you order 12 of each to start with. Then you can compare, their performance before you decide on the larger order. The extra speed of the V55 offers considerable advantages to some users, but to others (myself included) it is not necessary. Both systems are equally reliable.

I am happy to say that for large orders we do offer good disconts. I look forward to discussing this with you in due course.

When you do decide to place an order, please contact me personally by phone. I would like to make sure that we meet your requirements exactly.

If you have any further questions, please e-mail me again or phone me.

I look froward to hearing from you,

Best regards,

Linda Collins

2 **Discuss these questions:**
- How many mistakes did you find? What were they?
- How will Mr Martinez react to the e-mail? Will he place an order?

B **1** 👥 **Read this correspondence and decide on your answers to these questions:**
- What are the main points of each message? Highlight the main points.
- What needs to be included in the reply? Make notes on what you have to write.
- Which is the most urgent? Which should you answer first?

2 👤 **Write your replies to the correspondence.**

3 👤+👤 **Compare your replies with your partner's replies. What are the best points of each? Which of the replies would you prefer to receive?**

Dear –,

I visited your stand at the LanEx show in December and we talked about your products.

I gave you my business card and you promised to send me this season's catalogue, but I don't seem to have received it.

Could you please send me the latest catalogue and make sure that I am on your mailing list for future mailshots?

Yours sincerely,

Bill Young

Bill Young

Dear –,

I am making preparations for my visit to your office tomorrow.

I'm renting a car from the airport and will drive to you from there.

Can you tell me how long I should allow for the journey?

Is the office easy to find? If you could send me a sketch map to help me find my way, I would appreciate it.

I plan to be with you in time for lunch. May I invite you and your team to lunch? I have no idea about restaurants in your area, so could you book somewhere nice?

Looking forward to seeing you,

Best wishes,

Laura Thomas

Laura Thomas

Size [Medium ▲▼]   **B** *I* U T   [—]   [≣ ≣ ≣ ≣] [≣ ≣ ≣] [■]

Dear –,

RE: Purchase Order 336744

I am writing to find out why this order has not arrived.

I have tried phoning your Customer Services Department about this, but have been unable to talk to a real person. Sometimes the number is busy. Sometimes a recorded voice tells me to press several different keys. Then I have to listen to music, which is interrupted every 30 seconds by a voice saying, 'Thank you for waiting, we will be with you shortly.' So far I have waited for up to 30 minutes before hanging up. This is very frustrating.

I did manage to get through to your Sales Department earlier. They told me the goods were shipped on Tuesday and should have reached me on Wednesday. Then they put me back to Customer Services where I was kept on hold again until I had had enough.

This morning, Friday, I received an invoice for the goods, informing me that my credit card was charged on Tuesday. But I have not received the goods.

Please let me know what has happened to my order.

Regards,

James Nelson

16 I am sorry to inform you that . . .

Sorting out problems

A **1** Read this e-mail. What has happened? What does Bill have to do? How well do Mary and Bill know each other?

To: Bill Watts <bwatts@amicable.co.uk>
From: mary.fisher@solipsis.com

Bill,
I've discovered that the signed copy of your contract that you returned to us has been misplaced, so I'm afraid we'll have to send you another one to sign.

I really apologize. It's a mystery what's become of it. There's no problem at this point, but if you could return it to Laura Harris quickly, we'd really appreciate it. Thanks.

Regards,
Mary

2 Decide which of these phrases are FORMAL and which are INFORMAL.

introduction	I'm afraid I have some bad news . . . Due to circumstances beyond our control . . . I am sorry to inform you that . . . There's been a problem with . . .
apology	I am sorry for any inconvenience this has caused you. I apologize for the delay in shipping your order. I can assure you that this will not happen again. I'm really sorry about all this. Thanks for your help. Please let me know if there's anything I can do to help.

3 Imagine that Mary and Bill don't know each other well – rewrite the e-mail in A1 in a more formal style.

B **1** On Friday 13 February there was a small fire in your warehouse. The shipment for Ron Hernandez was damaged. It'll take another week to manufacture another batch. Make notes for the fax or e-mail you're going to send to Ron. Here is the original order he sent you:

Can I confirm this order which we discussed on the phone:

Quantity	Item	Size	Description	Unit price	Total price
250	1764	5 litre	Luxury strawberry ice cream	$1.98	$ 495
500	1891	10 litre	Soft vanilla ice cream	$3.47	$1735
				TOTAL	$2230

Please confirm that you can have this order ready for us to collect within the next three days.

2 Write a fax or e-mail to Ron to break the bad news. Apologize and explain what you're going to do. 'Send' it to another pair.

3 In the role of Ron Hernandez, reply to the fax or e-mail from the other pair. 'Send' the reply to them. Then read the reply you receive – is everything OK?

1 👥 On Friday, 13 March you placed an order by e-mail. Look at the notes on the right which you made before placing the order. Then check the confirmation below for mistakes.

2 👥 Write an e-mail to Chimera Paints to point out their mistakes and correct the order.

Order to Chimera Paints 13/03/01

7 x 5 litres

Cream vinyl @ € 73.95

5 x 1 litre

White gloss @ € 25.95

free shipping for e-mail orders

Inbox

✳ ❗ 🖉

From: support@chimera-farben.de To: smckinley@mckinley-and-wagstaff.com
Subject: Confirmation of Order 331379 Date: Sun, 21 Mar 01 23:33:55 +0000

Dear Mr McKinley,

Thank you for placing an order with Chimera Paints.

Your order number is 331379.

The items you have ordered are the following:

qty	size	type	colour	unit price	total
14	2.5 litres	Vinyl	Arctic White	€ 44.95	€ 629.30
2	2.5 litres	Gloss	Dorset Cream	€ 55.25	€ 110.50
				VAT @ 14.5%	€ 107.27
				Shipping	€ 50.00
				TOTAL	€ 897.07

Your credit card has been charged a total of € 899.07.

We have your shipping address as the following:

Mr Steve McKinley
McKinley and Wagstaff Ltd
Fitzharris Avenue
Denton DN7 9PQ

Shipping will normally take 1-2 weeks.
You can check the progress of your order at http://www.chimera-farben.de/ord/ordenq.asp

If any of the above details are incorrect please contact us immediately at
support@chimera-farben.de

Thank you for buying from Chimera.

Henry Mueller, European Sales Manager

---

3 👥👥 Look at each other's e-mails. Then discuss these questions:

- How could your e-mails be improved?
- Can you think of any problems you've had to sort out in writing? What did you do?
- What can you do if a client is rude to you?
- What extra difficulties will there be in real life, which didn't happen in this lesson?

"Did you get my e-mail?"

17 Can I ask some questions?

Asking questions and giving answers • Speaking politely

A **1** Look at the photos and discuss these questions:
- What do you think the relationship between the people in each photo is?
- What might they be talking about? What questions could they be asking?
- Which work situations cause people to ask questions most?

2 Look at the questions in this conversation. Complete the questions to match the answers:

Who *did you meet yesterday* ?	I met Mr Black.
When ?	We met at 11 a.m.
Where ?	We held it in the boardroom.
What ?	We talked about the next stage of the project.
What ?	He proposed delaying it for a month.
What ?	I said that wasn't necessary and he agreed.
What ?	We finished the meeting at 2:30.
Why ?	So early? He had a train to catch at 3.
How ?	I called him a taxi.

3 Listen to these phrases on the recording. Decide if the people asking and answering sound friendly and polite ✓ or unfriendly and rude ✗.

Can I ask some questions?		Yes, certainly.	
I'd like to ask some questions.		All right. What would you like to know?	
There are some questions I'd like to ask.		Of course. Go ahead.	
Could you tell me one more thing?		Sure.	
There's something else I'd like to know.		All right, how can I help?	
Sorry, could you say that again, please?		OK.	
Could I ask just one more question?		Certainly.	

Yes/No questions are not a good way of keeping a conversation going. Open questions, where the other person has to say more than just 'Yes' or 'No', are more effective.

But if you do ask a *Yes/No* question, a follow-up *Why?* question encourages the other person to say more.

B 1 Think of two people you know, e.g. business colleagues, clients or suppliers. Note down the following information about them. (If you can't think of anyone, invent two imaginary business associates.)

	Person A	Person B
Name		
Nationality and home town		
Job title		
Company and Department		
How often you see him/her		
What kind of relationship you have		
How long you've known him/her		
Where you first met him/her		

2 Ask questions (in a polite and friendly tone) to find out about your partner's business associates. Note down the information you get. Then check you have both noted the details down correctly.

C 1 One of you should look at File 12 on page 122, the other at File 43 on page 134. You'll take part in a telephone role play where you have to ask each other questions.

2 Discuss these questions:
- How would the situation you role-played be different in real life?
- In what business situations do people have to ask and answer lots of questions?
- How do you feel if someone talks to you in an unfriendly or rude voice?

The only way to get information from people is to ask them questions. Don't wait for them to tell you what you want to know – because they may not realize what you don't know. Most people like being asked questions because it helps them to find out what you need to know.

18 I'd like some more details . . .

Asking about details, specifications, numbers and prices

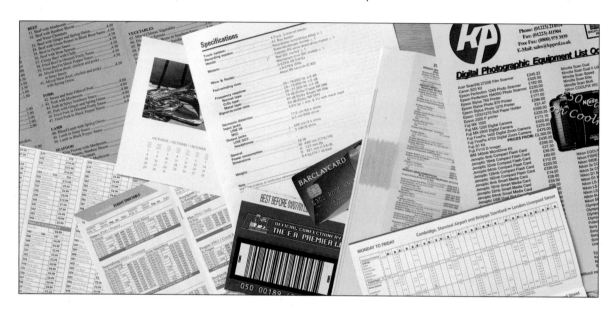

A

1 👥 **Look at the picture above. Can you identify where all the information might come from? Discuss these questions:**

- In your work, what kind of numbers might you have to deal with?
- In what situations might you need to listen to numbers being spoken?
  When might you say them aloud yourself. Think about dealing with colleagues and customers both face to face and over the phone.

2 🔊 **Listen to the recording and write the numbers in column A.**

		A	B
1	Phone number		
2	Fax number		
3	Reference number		
4	Bank account number		
5	Credit card number		
6	Invoice number		
7	Part number		
8	Customer number		

3 👥 **Check your answers in File 54 on page 138. Then change ONE digit in each number and dictate the new number to your partner and ask him or her to write the new number in column B. Then check that your partner has written down what you dictated.**

Do we say *dot*, *point*, *full stop* or *period*?

Say *dot*, if it's part of an e-mail and website address: *Amazon dot com*

Say *point* if it's a decimal point in calculations: *three times one point five is four point five*.

Say *full stop* (USA *period*) if it's a punctuation mark: *Put a full stop at the end of the sentence.*

Dot is often used for serial or catalogue numbers, but there are no fixed rules.

B

1 Some numbers, especially serial numbers, consist of letters, numbers and punctuation. Look at these examples – as you can see there are different ways of saying them.

Serial number: **120/AB–414.70G**

> *one two zero slash A B dash four one four dot seven zero G*

OR *one two O slash A B dash four one four dot seven O G*

Catalogue number: **334–AA–9987.34/Z**

> *three three four dash A A dash nine nine eight seven dot three four slash Z*

OR *three thirty-four dash double A dash ninety-nine eighty-seven dot thirty-four slash Z*

2 🔊 👥 Take turns to say the numbers on the labels aloud. Listen carefully to each other and check each other's pronunciation. Then listen to the model version.

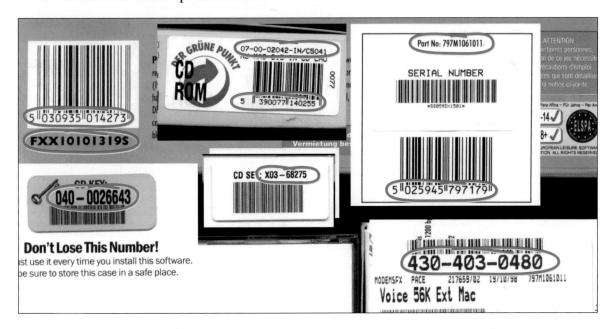

C

1 🔊 👥 Listen to these useful phrases for checking information and giving the requested information. Practise saying them.

Could you say that again, please?	*Yes, certainly . . .*
Hold on. I didn't get that.	*Oh, sorry. Let me repeat it.*
I'm sorry, what did you say?	*Oh, sorry. I'll say that again.*
Is that 334 or 344?	*Three three four*
Did you say 14 or 40?	*Fourteen – one four*
Is the last letter G or J?	*G for George*
Is that all OK?	*Can I just check if I've got everything right?*

2 👥 One of you should look at File 14 on page 123, the other at File 50 on page 137. You'll be taking part in a role play where you have to exchange information over the phone.

3 👥👥 Discuss these questions:

- Was the role play difficult or easy? Why?
- Do you feel under pressure when you make an overseas call? Why?
- What other kinds of information do you have to exchange over the phone?

19 Could you tell me more . . . ?

Asking follow-up questions • Answering difficult questions

A　**1**　👥　**Look at the picture. What kind of questions do you think the woman is asking?**

🔊　**Listen to their conversation and then discuss these questions:**

● What sort of person is Mr Grey? Why do you think he gives such short answers?
● How well did the woman deal with the situation? How did she feel, do you think?
● What would YOU say to Mr Grey?

2　👥　**Look at these questions and answers. What questions can you ask Mr Grey to find out more from him? Write your questions in the third column.**

Question	Answer	Follow-up question
Did you have a good journey?	Yes.	
Where do you come from?	England.	
Is this your first visit to our country?	No.	
How did you travel?	By plane.	
Did you have a good flight?	Not really.	
Is your hotel all right?	It's OK.	

3　🔊　👥　**Listen to Karen answering David's questions about a new product. Decide which follow-up question David should ask after each answer.**

1　Oh, we've spent a long time on it.
　　How long have you spent?　　　　　　　　How many people did you ask?

2　Six different colours, they said.
　　Which colours do they want?　　　　　　Why do they want six colours?

3　We discovered that if the price goes down by 20%, our sales will rise by 50%.
　　What if the price drops by 30%?　　　　What if we raise our prices?

4　Probably next year.
　　When exactly next year?　　　　　　　　Do you mean in the spring?

5　Yes, we do. It's the ZX 410.
　　Is it too late to come up with a better name?　　Why did you come up with that name?

B **1** **Listen to these phrases which you can use when you can't answer a question quickly. Practise saying them.**

gaining time to think	Mmm, let me see, . . . Well...um... Er...well... Yes, that's an interesting question. Well, . . .
delaying	Could I get back to you on that question? I need to find out the answer. Just a minute, I need to check that. I don't really want to give a quick answer to that. I need a little time to find out more. Can I get back to you with an answer? I'll have to check.
don't know	I'm afraid I can't answer that question. I really don't know, I'm afraid. I'm not really sure of the answer.

2 **One of you should look at File 17 on page 124, the other at File 48 on page 136. You'll be asking for information about products in your firm's catalogue.**

Here are some ways you can introduce your questions:

> Can I ask you a question about . . .?
> There are a couple of questions I'd like to ask you . . .
> There's something else I want to know.

3 **Write a reply to this e-mail from a client about the products in Files 17 and 48.**

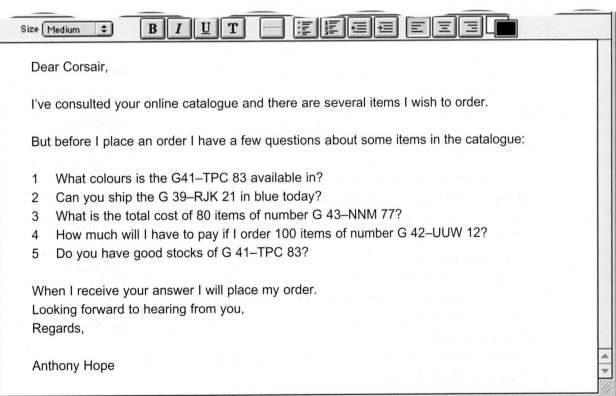

Size [Medium ▼] **B** *I* <u>U</u> **T**

Dear Corsair,

I've consulted your online catalogue and there are several items I wish to order.

But before I place an order I have a few questions about some items in the catalogue:

1 What colours is the G41–TPC 83 available in?
2 Can you ship the G 39–RJK 21 in blue today?
3 What is the total cost of 80 items of number G 43–NNM 77?
4 How much will I have to pay if I order 100 items of number G 42–UUW 12?
5 Do you have good stocks of G 41–TPC 83?

When I receive your answer I will place my order.
Looking forward to hearing from you,
Regards,

Anthony Hope

20 When can we meet?

Arranging appointments and meetings

A 1 Listen to Terry Hughes talking to his assistant about what he's doing on Monday and Tuesday. Add the missing information to his diary.

Monday 1st

9:00	Work on report for Mr Pearson
11:00	Meet _____
12:30	Lunch with Ms Ford at _____
14:30	Remember to _____
_____	Report due for Mr Pearson
18:00	Betty Dixon calling from _____

Tuesday 2nd

_____	Brainstorming meeting with Marketing staff
11:15	Anne-Marie from _____ arrives
12:00	_____ with Anne-Marie
13:00	Lunch at Lorenzo's with Anne-Marie, _____ and _____
15:30	Meeting with Nancy and Mark _____
16:00	_____

Wednesday 3rd

8:30	Call Mr Fujimoto in Yokohama
10:30	Jean-Pierre from Paris office arrives
11:30	Meeting with Export team (boardroom)
12:30	Jean-Pierre & team: working lunch (canteen)
15:00	~~New products presentation~~ CANCELLED
17:30	Call Hank Turner in Dallas
20:00	Opera with Jean-Pierre (dinner after at Sukho Thai restaurant)

Thursday 4th

8:00	Call Mr Kim in Seoul
9:00	Jochen Müller from Stuttgart arrives
11:00	Meeting with Jochen and European team leaders (Meeting Room 3)
13:00	Meeting with Liz Thompson (sandwiches)
15:00	~~Meeting with Tim~~ CANCELLED
14:30	Leave for airport for flight to Stuttgart (with Jochen)

---

2 Take turns to play the roles of Terry and Chris, a colleague.

Student A

1 You are Chris. Ask questions to find out what Terry's plans are for Wednesday.

2 Change roles. Now you are Terry. Answer Chris's questions.

Student B

1 You are Terry. Answer Chris's questions by consulting your diary above.

2 Change roles. Now you are Chris. Find out what Terry's plans are for Thursday.

B 1 Listen to these phrases which you can use when arranging an appointment or meeting. Practise saying them.

> Are you free on Monday?
>
> Are you available on Tuesday?
>
> How much time do you have for a meeting on Wednesday?
>
> How long do you think we need to discuss this?
>
> Do you have any time for a meeting on Wednesday?
>
> Are you free for lunch on Monday?

> I'm free from 4 till 5 on Monday.
>
> I'm busy all day on Tuesday.
>
> I'm free all morning. How long do we need?
>
> Half an hour is enough, I think.
>
> I don't have any time at all on Wednesday, but I could manage Monday after lunch.
>
> Yes, I'm free then. Let's have lunch together!

2 Take turns to play each role in this phone conversation. Some of the phrases above may be useful.

You may find it helpful to go through it together deciding exactly what you're going to say, before you actually begin the role play.

> **You are Eddie. Call Nicky and explain you want to arrange a meeting for next week.**

> **You are Nicky. Answer the phone and say you're free on Monday.**

> **Say you're busy on Monday, but free on Tuesday.**

> **Ask if Tuesday afternoon is OK.**

> **Say that 3 pm is fine.**

> **Find out where the meeting will be.**

> **Say the meeting will be in your office.**

> **Agree to this. But say that you have to catch a train at 5 pm.**

> **Say that an hour is long enough.**

> **Ask Eddie to e-mail you an agenda.**

> **Agree to do this tomorrow.**

C 1 One of you should look at File 18 on page 124, the other at File 49 on page 136. You'll be arranging THREE meetings next week.

2 + Discuss these questions:

- Did you make the same decisions about when and where to meet?
- If there are differences, why did you make the decisions you made?
- In business, what other factors do you take into account when arranging a meeting or appointment?

21 Avoiding misunderstandings

Dealing with cultural differences

 A 1 **Look at the photos and discuss these questions:**
- Which countries do you think the people come from?
- How do business people greet each other in your country when they first meet?
- How do they greet each other when they know each other well?

2 **Listen to two business travellers talking about things they did wrong when on business abroad. Match the advice they give to the countries on the right.**

1 Don't criticize people or embarrass them, and avoid confrontation.	Brazil
2 Don't keep your left hand in your pocket when shaking hands.	Britain
3 Don't refer to the UK as England or to the British as English.	France
4 Don't use first names unless you are invited to.	Germany
5 Eye contact conveys sincerity and attentiveness to the speaker.	Italy
6 Greet a stranger by saying your name, not 'How do you do?'	Japan
7 Men touch each other in a friendly way, so don't try to move away.	Korea
8 Shake hands firmly because a weak handshake is a sign of weakness.	Mexico
9 Shake hands with everyone in the group when you arrive.	Russia
10 Shake hands with everyone in the group when you leave.	Scotland
11 Hold business cards with both hands and read them carefully.	Taiwan
12 Too much eye contact may embarrass people.	USA

3 **Compare your answers. Which of the advice would you also give to visitors to your country? Which advice would you not give?**

Some rules about dealing with people from different cultures:
- Recognize that cultural diversity exists.
- Show respect for people as unique individuals and respect for the unfamiliar.
- Be willing to modify your own performance according to the other person's cultural background.
  (But don't try to copy their behaviour because this may be embarrassing.)

B 1 👥 **Look at these situations and discuss these questions about each one:**
- Why does each misunderstanding happen?
- What should each person do and say?
- What do people in your country do in this situation?
- How is your own attitude different from the attitudes of each person?

First names

Herr Doktor Berger from Germany gets upset when Hank Carter from the USA keeps calling him Heinrich. He is so angry that he finishes the meeting early.

Personal questions

When Don Smith first meets WJ Chang from Taiwan, he is embarrassed to be asked 'Are you married?' and 'What's your blood type?'

Hugs and kisses

José Garcia from Spain got to know his Korean counterpart Hyun Kim Lee very well. When he meets her again, he gives her a hug and kisses her on the cheek. She is terribly embarrassed.

Titles

When Diplomingenieur Hans Weiss from Austria visits Australia, he tells people his name and title. He is upset when they smile. They seem to be making fun of him.

Silence

Bill Brown from the UK is in a meeting with Mr Tanaka in Japan. There are long silences during the meeting so Bill keeps finding things to say. Mr Tanaka thinks he is a rather unintelligent person.

Time

Monsieur Leroi from France arrives late for his 3 pm meeting with Tina Webb from the USA. She was on time and is annoyed. The meeting is due to end at 5 pm and she insists on ending then. He is upset.

2 👥 **What advice would you give to a first-time foreign visitor to your country? Add three DOS and three DON'TS to this list:**

Do . . .

carry business cards and give them to people you meet – they will help people to remember your name and find out what your job is.

....

....

....

Don't . . .

talk about politics and religion – these subjects are considered personal and sensitive.

....

....

....

3 👥 + 👥 **Compare your DOS and DON'TS. Which is the most useful piece of advice?**

⭐ It's not just people from different <u>countries</u> who behave differently.

People in different regions of the same country behave differently. People of different ages behave differently. People with different education behave differently. Friends behave differently from acquaintances. Men behave differently from women.

Every individual person behaves differently.

22 Thank you for your order . . .

Dealing with problems with orders

A 1 **You work in the sales department of Portico Products, which manufactures garden and beach furniture. Listen to some customers placing orders over the phone. One piece of information is unclear in each call. Which question would you ask each person?**

1 . . . because that's how many we need.
Did you say 50 or 15?   Why do you need so many?

2 . . . get this order processed as soon as possible.
Which order do you mean?   Is that the 19th of this month or next month?

3 . . . there will be two truck loads, but that's OK.
Can we deliver on Saturday?   Do you want them shipped to the factory or warehouse?

4 . . . needs to be written on the shipping note.
How do you spell the name of the consignee?   Is that Ms or Mrs?

5 . . . so he didn't find the right building.
Is that Richmond Road or Richmond Avenue?   How do you spell 'Richmond'?

6 . . . you'll need that for the invoice if you're mailing it.
Who should we send the invoice to?   Is the postal code 89372 or 89732?

7 . . . have them here as soon as possible.
How can we get them to you quickly?   Shall we deliver them or can you collect them?

8 . . . Can you do that?
What is the total quantity you require?   Do you only want 30 this time?

2 Compare your answers.

B 1 **You work together in the sales department of Portico Products. Read the fax opposite from a valued customer. Then check your inventory on the computer (below the fax). Decide together what you are going to say to Mr Tucker. Then write a reply to him.**

48

Arcadia
Hotel and Leisure Group
100 Beach Road EMPYRIA

1st February 20–

Dear Alex,

Thank you sending us your catalogue and price lists.

I'd like to place an order for the following:

quantity	product	colour	unit price	total price
80	Dinna dining chairs	red	€ 12	€ 960
20	Rondda round tables	white	€ 95	€ 1900
25	Flopp reclining chairs	white	€ 75	€ 1875
12	Sitta armchairs	yellow	€ 55	€ 660
6	Likka footstools	yellow	€ 13	€ 78
5	Summa parasols	rainbow	€ 45	€ 225
5	Uppa parasol bases	green	€ 8	€ 40
			total	€ 5738

Our summer season begins on 1 May but we require delivery by <u>30 March</u> because our staff need time to assemble the units and set them up in our various sites.

Looking forward to hearing from you,

Don Tucker
Leisure Club Director

Inventory

Product	Colour	Quantity in stock	Next run + date	Price	
Flopp reclining chairs	white	20	400 (April 2)	€ 75	
	green	100	200 (May 1)	€ 60	¶¶
Sitta armchairs	yellow	7	300 (March 15)	€ 55	
	white	298	none	€ 50	¶¶
Likka footstools	white	185	none	€ 13	
	yellow	45	none	€ 13	
Dinna dining chairs	white	2	replaced by Snakka	€ 12	
	red	4	replaced by Snakka	€ 12	
Snakka dining chairs	red	86	600 (June 2)	€ 15	
Rondda round tables	white	9	100 (April 15)	€ 90	¶¶
	cream	189	none	€ 90	¶¶
Summa parasols	green	55	100 (April 4)	€ 40	¶¶
	rainbow	4	100 (April 4)	€ 40	¶¶
Uppa parasol bases	green	33	none	€ 6	¶¶

¶¶ indicates price change since catalogue was published

Allow 10 days for shipping
20% discount for orders over € 5000, 10% discount for orders over € 3000

2 Look at **File 64** on page 142 to see Mr Tucker's reply. Write back to Mr Tucker.
When you have written your reply to Mr Tucker, look at **File 33** on page 130.

3 👥 + 👥 Compare your experiences and ask the other pair these questions:
- What did you write to Mr Tucker in **B1**? What surprised you about his reply?
- In real life, how would the situation be different?

23 What are your views?

Different kinds of meetings • Discussing ideas and exchanging opinions

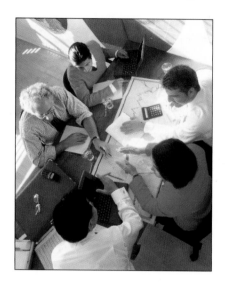

A 1 **Look at the photos and discuss these questions:**

- How are the two meetings in the photos different?
- Have you had experience of the two kinds of meetings?
- Which would you prefer to attend?
- What do you like *and* dislike about meetings in general?

2 Read this extract from a training book about meetings. Then look at 3 and 4 opposite.

Why do business people have meetings?

A meeting is when two or more people agree to assemble in the same room. Most meetings are planned in advance. They usually have an agenda or schedule. They take place without interruptions from phone calls and visitors.

A small group or one-to-one meeting is often less formal than a larger meeting. A larger meeting has one person in the chair who controls the group, asks participants to speak and makes sure they stick to the agenda – and finish on time.

Meetings are held for different purposes:

1 Dealing with information

A meeting is a good way of informing everyone about a new policy or a new product. It gives people a chance to ask questions, give their reactions in public and discuss problems that arise. A team may meet to find out what progress each member has made. A group of managers may meet to establish consensus, making sure everyone is informed and can ask questions before further action is taken. In this kind of meeting people give reports, explain changes, give feedback and ask questions.

2 Resolving problems

Different people's points of view can help to find a solution to a problem. The participants may have to reach a compromise before agreement is reached.

3 Making decisions

If major decisions have to be made, this process can be shared between the people in a meeting. The alternative is for one manager to make big decisions as well as smaller day-to-day decisions. In this kind of meeting the participants may be presented with options to choose between.

4 Encouraging ideas

A meeting is a good way of brainstorming solutions to a difficult problem. Each participant has different views which he or she can share with the others. Other people's ideas often stimulate new ideas.

3 👥 Match these examples to one or more of the kinds of meeting mentioned in the extract.

a Everyone suggests different ideas for marketing a product.
b Managers and staff talk about allocating car parking spaces.
c People find out about the progress of a project.
d Staff and managers talk about pay or conditions.
e A supplier talks to a buyer about products in the catalogue.

4 👥 Discuss these questions:

● Which parts of the text do you disagree with?
● How are meetings in your company and country different from the ones described in the text?

B **1** 🔊 👥 Listen to these phrases and practise saying them. Which would you ONLY say at an informal meeting and when talking to someone you are good friends with?

asking for views	Yes, John? / John, what do you think?
	John, what are your views? / John, are you asleep?
giving your view	I think we should . . . / The best thing to do is . . .
	Why don't we . . . ? / One thing we could do is . . .
agreeing	That's right. / I have nothing to add, really.
	I agree with what Mary said. / Yes. That's true.
disagreeing	I don't quite agree that . . . / That's wrong.
	All right, but don't you think that . . . ? / I don't agree with you.
	I see what you mean, but . . . / That's not right.

2 👥👥 Sit in a circle or face each other across a table.
Imagine that you are taking part in a business meeting. Make
sure each of you has at least one turn to chair the 'meeting'.

Chairperson: Ask everyone to look at one of these cuttings.
Ask them for their views and make sure everyone has a chance to speak.

Everyone else: Give your views and react to the others' opinions.

Happy workers work harder

AN OFFICE full of people who laugh and joke and have fun is more productive. Business shouldn't be taken too seriously, according to a report from

Shorter vacations increase productivity

Companies where workers get two weeks vacation are more productive than firms where they get four weeks. This is what a report from

Retirement age to rise to 70

The Government is about to announce that the age of retirement for men and women is going up to 70 next year. The average age of the population

Teleworking saves companies money

With more staff working at home office buildings are getting smaller and companies are saving on rent, heating and other costs. When

3 👥👥 Discuss these questions:

● When you chaired the 'meeting', what did you find difficult?
● Did everyone get a chance to give their point of view? If not, why not?
● In a real meeting, what would be different?

24 Thank you for coming!

Participating in one-to-one meetings

(A)

1 👥 Look at how the people in the photos are sitting. How do you think seating arrangements might affect the behaviour of the people at each meeting? Which arrangement would you find most suitable for a business meeting?

2 🔊 We talked to two business people before and after a meeting. First, listen to them talking before their meetings. Put S next to the things that Sarah expects to happen in her meeting, and C next to the things Carlos expects to happen in his meeting.

.... It will be a routine meeting.   .... We are unlikely to disagree.

.... It will be an easy meeting.   .... We are likely to disagree.

.... It will be a difficult meeting.   .... We will be giving each other information.

.... It will be an enjoyable meeting.   .... I'm going to take notes.

.... There will be two of us at the meeting.   .... The other person is going to take notes.

.... There will be three of us at the meeting.   .... It will finish early.

      .... It will overrun.

3 🔊 Now listen to Sarah's and Carlos's reports. Which of their predictions came true?

4 👥 Compare your answers. Then discuss:

- Which of these meetings have you attended recently? What happened?
  performance appraisal   training   project planning and scheduling   project update
  project review   other

⭐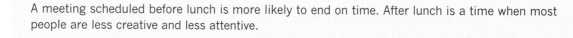
A meeting scheduled before lunch is more likely to end on time. After lunch is a time when most people are less creative and less attentive.

B 1 🔊 Listen to the beginning and end of an informal one-to-one meeting. Which of these phrases did the participants use? Tick the phrases they used.

socializing	How was your holiday?	☐
	Are you going away this summer?	☐
	Where would you like to sit?	☐
starting	OK. Shall we start?	☐
	Now, then, the first thing we need to talk about . . .	☐
	I'd like to talk about . . .	☐
ending	Is there anything else you'd like to discuss?	☐
	Is there anything we've forgotten?	☐
	So, we agree that . . .	☐
	So, you're going to . . . and I'm going to . . .	☐
next meeting	Let's meet again next month.	☐
	Right, what date would suit you?	☐

2 👥 Play the roles of host and visitor in this role play, using some of the phrases above.

Host	**Visitor**
Welcome your visitor, offer a seat.	
	Thank your host.
Ask about his/her recent holiday.	
	Say it was cancelled – now you're going next week. Ask about your host's holiday plans.
Say you have no plans. Begin the meeting.	
	Say you have to leave at 5 pm.

Imagine that the meeting has continued till 5 pm . . .

Host	**Visitor**
Say it's nearly 5 o'clock.	
	Ask if everything has been covered.
You think so. Arrange another meeting.	
	Next month on the 15th?
Agree, thank him/her for coming.	
	Thank him/her for the meeting. Say goodbye.

C 1 👥 One of you should look at File 19 on page 125, the other at File 53 on page 138. You'll be taking part in another one-to-one meeting – this time including the main discussion phase.

2 👥 + 👥 Discuss these questions:
- What happened in your meeting? Did you reach agreement? If not, why not?
- In a real meeting, what would be different?

25 The first item on the agenda is . . .

Working with an agenda • Taking part in larger meetings with a chairperson

 1 👥 **Look at the photo and discuss these questions:**

- What kind of meeting is going on in the picture?
- What are the documents on the table?
- What does the chairperson at a meeting like this do?
- When did you last attend a meeting like this? What happened?

2 🔊 👥 **Listen to a phone call. Mike is asking Sue to change some items on the agenda for the meeting. Make the changes they agree to.**

Project teams meeting
Central Office Boardroom
15 January 09:00 for 09:15

Chair: Michael Roberts   Secretary: Sue Robinson
Members: DE, JK, NM, SMcK, LJ, AWC, NB, CA, SMG, ZJ, TMJ, CM

1	09:15	Matters arising from last meeting
2	09:30	Report from Dan Evans on Monaco project
3	09:50	Discussion of Monaco project
4	10:00	Presentation on new San Marino products (Julie King and Nancy Moore)
5	10:30	Presentation on changes to export procedures (Carlo Marinelli)
	11:00	Coffee break
6	11.30	Teams meet in Meeting Rooms 2, 4 and 5 (separate agendas)
7	13:00	Reports from teams
8	14:00	Any other business
9	14:15	Details of next meeting
	14:20	Lunch in canteen (13 people)

3 👥 **Compare your answers. Then discuss these questions:**

- Why do meetings have an agenda?
- Should people at a meeting keep to the times on the agenda? Or should it be flexible?
- Do the meetings you attend usually end on time? Why/Why not?

B 1 🔊 Look at these phrases you can use in a formal meeting. Listen to the recording and write *C* beside the phrases that were used by the chairperson and *P* beside the ones the participants used.

starting	*Good morning everyone. Welcome.*	....
	If you have a mobile phone, could you please turn it off?	....
	Shall we begin?	....
	Has everyone got a copy of the agenda?	....
	All right. Now, the first item on the agenda is . . .	....
managing the meeting	*Does anyone have any questions before we move on?*	....
	Could you answer that for us?	....
	Thank you everyone. Now, shall we move on to the next point?	....
suggesting	*Could I make a suggestion?*	....
asking	*Could I ask a question, please?*	....
interrupting	*Sorry, could I interrupt for a moment?*	....
	Could I just say something?	....
ending	*Well, we're nearly out of time. Can we come to a conclusion?*	....
	So, what we have decided is . . .	....
	So do we all agree that . . .?	....
	Well, thank you very much, everyone.	....
	We'll meet again on the 11th of next month at 2 o'clock.	....

2 👥 Each of you should look at a different file: one at File 5 on page 119, one at File 36 on page 131, and one at File 39 on page 132.

You'll be taking part in a FORMAL meeting with one person in the chair. Begin by deciding who is going to chair the meeting.

Before you start the meeting, look at this agenda. How long is your meeting going to last?

> **Project: SPECTRUM Mark 2 Progress Meeting**
>
> 1 Report from Design Team
> 2 Report from Production Team
> 3 Report from Sales Team
> 4 Discussion of reports
> 5 The way ahead
> 6 Any other business

3 👥 Form a group with students who were in a different meeting just now. Discuss these questions:

- What happened in your meeting?
- What decisions were reached?
- What did you find most difficult in the meeting?
- What have you learned from doing this role play?

 In a meeting, listen carefully to what the other people say. React to what they say. Don't just sit there deciding what you're going to say and waiting for a chance to say it.

26 We need to come to an agreement

Taking part in negotiations

A **1** Read this text about negotiation. Fill the blanks in the text with words from this list:

agreement • bargaining • compromise • concessions • deadlock
gain • offers • priorities • reactions

Why do business people negotiate?

A negotiation is a way of reaching an agreement by means of discussion and _____ . Each side has something the other wants and both sides are trying to reach an agreement. Negotiators bargain with each other as they make _____ ("We will ... if you ...?") and ask for _____ ("If we ..., will you ...?"). Negotiators don't enter a negotiation expecting to get everything they want, they know they'll have to _____ . If they don't, there will be _____ and the negotiation will break down.

The purpose of every negotiation is to reach an agreement. Usually both sides are meeting because they have something to _____ . In a sales negotiation, the seller wants to sell the goods or services and the buyer wants to buy them. In a pay negotiation, the employer wants the workers to work and the workers want to work. Both sides want to reach an _____ , but they have different _____ .

A long, important negotiation is conducted differently from a smaller, less important one, but most negotiations include these stages:

1 Preparation	Both sides decide what they want, and prioritize their wants. They anticipate the other side's _____ and decide what concessions they can make.
2 Proposal	Each side explains its proposal: *Our proposal is . . .*
3 Debate	The sides discuss the proposals: *Can you explain why . . . ?*
4 Bargaining	The sides make or ask for concessions: *If we agree to . . . , are you prepared to . . . ?*
5 Closing	The sides reach an agreement: *Do we have a deal then?*

2 Discuss these questions:

- How are the negotiations in your company and in your country different from the ones described in the text?
- What everyday examples of negotiations can you think of, e.g. deciding who is going to do the chores at home – and when?

3 Which of these negotiations have you taken part in? Describe what happened.

- buying something in a market
- a commercial business negotiation
- buying/selling something second-hand
- persuading a co-worker to help you with a time-consuming task
- convincing your office manager to give you an extra bookshelf or new computer
- asking your manager for a day off at short notice

B 1 🔊 👥 **Listen to Kevin and Donna negotiating the installation of a new ventilation system. Complete this table to show who makes each suggestion and if the other agrees.**

Suggestion	Who suggests this?	Does the other agree?

Installation
  this month
  during the day
  at night so as not to disrupt office
  at the weekend
	....
	 ....
	 ....
	 ....
		....
		 ....
		 ....
		 ....

Maintenance
  free maintenance for the first 12 months
  service contract for the following year
  maintenance at cost for the following year
	....
	 ....
	 ....
		....
		 ....
		 ....

2 👥 **Compare your answers. What did you think of the negotiators' performances?**

 C 1 🔊 **Listen to these phrases which you can use in a negotiation. Practise saying them.**

proposing	Can I just begin by outlining our proposal? The advantages of our proposal are . . .
reacting	One of the problems I can foresee is . . . I can see the advantages, but from our point of view . . . It's difficult for us to . . .
bargaining	Maybe we could increase the size of our order. Could you reduce the price by . . . ? Delivering by May 30 is difficult for us. Maybe we could ship in two batches? We do need to get it installed by the end of May. Could you do it on the 28th?
ending	That seems fine. We seem to be agreed. I'll put something in writing by the end of the week and send it to you.

2 👥 + 👥 **Two of you should look at File 21 on page 126, the others at File 55 on page 139. You'll be taking part in a role play about the purchase of equipment.**

3 👥👥 **Form a group with students who were in different groups in C2. Discuss these questions:**

- What happened in your negotiation? What concessions did you make?
- Did both sides leave the negotiation feeling satisfied? If not, why not?
- What are some of the differences between a real-life negotiation and the role play?

www.CartoonStock.com

27 When does 'Yes' mean 'Yes'?

Different styles of negotiating

A **1** **Look at the photo and discuss these questions:**

- Which country do you think the photo shows? Why?
- When are humour and jokes appropriate in meetings in your country?

2 🔊 **You'll hear two experienced businessmen talking about negotiating around the world. First listen to Charles Cotton and write America or Asia beside the summaries of what he said.**

People need to build a personal relationship before they trust each other. ....

They trust the companies the others represent. ....

Reaching agreement might take two weeks. ....

Reaching agreement might take two months. ....

3 🔊 **Now listen to Peter Callaghan and write Europe or Australia beside the summaries of what he said.**

People first outline what they want to achieve. ....

People soon begin to discuss the points they need to compromise on. ....

It takes a long time to explain what you want to achieve. ....

It doesn't take long to explain what you want to achieve. ....

If you make a mistake, you lose face. ....

Making a mistake doesn't matter too much. ....

People don't want to commit themselves too soon. ....

It's OK to change your mind about a decision after a meeting. ....

4 **Decide which of these statements are true about doing business and negotiating in your country. Tick the true statements.**

1 Meetings start and end on time.

Meetings start 10–15 minutes late but end on time.

Meetings start late and they overrun.

2 Participants show most respect to the oldest person present.

Participants show respect to the most senior person present.

Everyone is equal in a meeting.

3 People get upset if they lose face.

People will stop co-operating if they have lost face.

Losing face is less important than losing business.

4 People prefer not to talk business over a meal.

People expect to talk business over a meal.

It's OK to talk business over lunch, but not dinner.

5 Jokes make people feel uncomfortable at meetings.

Humour and jokes help people to feel more relaxed.

Humour has no place in business.

5 👥👥 **Compare your answers. Then discuss these questions:**
- Which points that Charles and Peter made are also true about your country?
- What would you tell an American and a British person about meetings and negotiations in your country?

B **1** 👥👥 **Imagine that you're hosting a one-day conference for colleagues from other branches of your company. They come from the Japanese, American, Mexican and British branches – and choose one other nationality to invite. This will be their first visit to your country.**

Role-play a preliminary meeting to prepare for the conference.
Discuss the questions on this agenda.
One of you should chair the meeting.

> **AGENDA**
>
> **1.** What are we going to do to make everyone feel at home?
>
> **2.** How are we going to arrange the seating in the meeting room?
>
> **3.** What are the visitors going to find strange about the way people in our country behave?
>
> **4.** What individual advice are we going to give to each nationality?
>
> **5.** What kind of food and refreshments are we going to offer?

2 **Give a report to the rest of the class on your meeting.**

3 **Write a short report, summarizing the decisions you made at your meeting.**

⭐ Don't assume that everyone from a country behaves in the same way. Generalizations about national characteristics are obviously untrue – not *all* British people spend their time talking about the weather! There's no such thing as a typical British person or a typical American. Every individual is different. And times change – business people don't behave in the same way as they did twenty years ago.

FREQUENT FLYER CLASS (EXCUSED SAFETY DEMO)

28 We need to meet . . .

Simulating a series of meetings

A 1 👥 Bobo is a world-famous TV character who appeals to children and adults alike. You work for Bobo International Merchandising (BIM), a company that produces goods based on the Bobo characters. Read the e-mail from your director and the flyer about Bobo products. Then discuss the questions opposite.

Size | Medium ▾ | **B** *I* U̲ T — ≣ ≣ ≣ ≣ ≣ ≣ ≣ ■

"Bobo and His Friends" is set to be the most popular children's TV show next year. Our current range of merchandise is quite small, but there is a big demand for more products, which will be bought by parents for their young children, by older children with their pocket money, and by enthusiastic adult fans. The number of adult fans is increasing by 50% each year, so this is an important and potentially profitable market.

Please get back to me with your ideas for new products.

Toni Andres
Director-General

Good news from BOBO AND HIS FRIENDS

Bobo has never been more popular. This is why your store can make your customers happy by stocking Bobo products, available now from BIM.

Some of our products are designed for youngsters – the people who watch Bobo on TV every morning.

Some are designed for adults – Bobo's growing army of fans.

But most are suitable for all Bobo fans – from age 1 to 81!

So join us in celebrating the success of Bobo and share our success by deciding to stock Bobo products. Your customers will say Thank You and they'll come back for more.

2 Discuss these questions:

- Why are characters like Pingu, Mickey Mouse and Bugs Bunny popular?
- Why do you think characters like Bobo are popular with adults as well as children?
- Who is your favourite character? Do/Would you buy things with his/her logo on?

B The class is divided into three teams. Each team should work in a separate area of the room.

1 Each team has a different task. Hold a brainstorming meeting to come up with ideas.

Team A	Team B	Team C
Your task is to come up with 4 new **BOBO** products for young children. Here are some ideas to start you thinking . . . breakfast cereal videos bath foam birthday cards . . . now come up with some more ideas of your own!	Your task is to come up with 4 new **BOBO** products for teenagers and adults. Here are some ideas to start you thinking . . . computer mouse mobile phone cover mouse mat computer game . . . now come up with some more ideas of your own!	Look at the existing products on the flyer. Your task is to decide . . . which to promote which to discontinue which to redesign. If there's time, try to think of some new products, developed from the existing ones.

2 You have received this agenda from head office. Read it through and decide what your team is going to say at each stage of the meeting – and/or think of questions to ask.

One representative from each team will attend the meeting.

AGENDA

1. Comments on existing range
2. Products for children
3. Products for adults
4. Cross-over products for all ages
5. Ideas for other promotional activities
6. The future for Bobo products

C **1** Form groups of three with a member from Team A, B and C in each. Decide who will chair the meeting.

2 After the meeting, discuss these questions as a whole class:

- What did you find difficult about the meeting?
- Did you manage to have your say? If not, why not?
- What would you do differently if you had the meeting again?

29 Make yourself at home!

Receiving visitors • Making people feel at home • Giving and receiving gifts

A 1 **Look at the photos and discuss these questions:**

● What parts of the world do you think the photos show?
● How do you greet the following people? What difference does it make if they are male or female?
  – a new business acquaintance
  – an old business friend
  – a colleague from a foreign branch of your company

2 🔊 **Listen to Bob Campbell welcoming Corinne Fulbert to his office in Canada. Note down your answers to these questions.**

1 How well do they know each other?
2 When did Corinne's plane land?
3 Why has she arrived late at Bob's office?

4 What gift does she give him?
5 What does he say that upsets her?

3 🔊 👥 **Imagine that you're Bob and you're visiting Corinne in France for the first time. Think of replies to these remarks from your host. Think of more to say than just *Yes* or *Yes, please*. Then compare your replies with the model version on the recording.**

Hello, Bob. It's really nice to see you again.

Did you have a good journey?

Can I take your coat?

Do you need to freshen up?

Would you like something to drink?

I've booked lunch for 1 o'clock. Is that OK?

Are you booked into a hotel tonight?

Would you like me to show you around the factory?

Would you like Tim to look after your bag till later?

B ⵌⵌ In your country, do business people give gifts when they visit each other? Look at this information. Then discuss the questions below.

In Japan if you receive a gift, take it with both hands and open it later in private. If you give a gift (such as something from your country), it must be wrapped beautifully.

In Germany if you're invited to someone's house, buy flowers for the hostess. Remove the wrapping before handing them to her.

In Cuba if you receive a gift, open it right away while the other person is watching.

In Korea it is good manners to refuse a gift at first – people have to be persuaded to accept one.

In Russia male and female visitors are often given a bunch of flowers to welcome them.

In Taiwan give your gift with both hands. Don't give clocks, towels, knives, letter-openers, scissors, or white, blue or black items. If someone gives you a gift, open it later in private.

In the UK it's not customary to give gifts. But if you go to someone's home, take a bottle of wine or some flowers.

- What advice would you give about giving gifts and receiving gifts in your country?
- What kinds of gifts do people in your country give when visiting someone's home?
- What kinds of gifts would you take on a business trip?
- How might the other person feel . . .
    . . . if you gave something too expensive   . . . or too cheap
    . . . or if you gave nothing?

The perfect gift? Something small and tasteful is better than something large and expensive. Maybe some typical food or drink from your country (e.g. Belgian chocolates from Belgium, wine from France or Germany), or a nicely-wrapped product from your country (e.g. a fountain pen, a crystal glass). Nice wrapping paper is important, too.

Best of all, give something you know the other person will really appreciate (e.g. a CD if she loves music or a book if he likes to read).

Bad colours for gift wrapping: purple in Mexico, yellow in Russia, white, blue or black in Taiwan, black and white in Japan, black or purple in Brazil.

C 1 ⵌ Imagine you're the host. How would you reply to these remarks from your visitor?

Well, here I am at last. I didn't think I'd make it.

What a terrible journey!

Can I just freshen up before we start?

I'm really thirsty. Could I get something to drink?

I've brought you a small gift. I hope you like it.

Could I just make a quick phone call to my office?

Is there somewhere I can leave my bag till later?

Can I just phone my hotel?

Could I have a tour of the factory at some stage?

2 ⵌ One of you should look at **File 22** on page 126, the other at **File 56** on page 139. You'll be playing the roles of visitor and host.

30 What shall we talk about?

Small talk • Socializing • Building professional relationships

A 1 👥 **Look at the photo and discuss these questions:**

- When do/will you have to socialize with business associates in English? Number these situations to show when you (will) have to socialize most (**1**) and least (**10**):

  .... before getting down to business   .... during the day over coffee or tea
  .... at lunchtime   .... in the evening over drinks
  .... in the evening in a restaurant   .... at your or the other person's home
  .... at the weekend   .... travelling together
  .... before a meeting or presentation   .... at a sporting event

- What do you enjoy about socializing with business associates from your own country?
- Apart from having to talk in English, what do you find difficult about socializing with foreign people?

2 🔊 👥 **Jim and Emma are business associates. This is the first time they have travelled together. Listen to two versions of the same situation. Then discuss these questions:**

- Why is the second version of their conversation better than the first?
- How do they encourage each other to continue in the second version?
- What questions do they ask each other in the second version?

Socializing is necessary in business if you want to build a relationship with someone. A good relationship can help you to do business more easily – and it's more rewarding to deal with people you know than with strangers. A good personal relationship creates a stronger business relationship.

Many business people find socializing more difficult than a business meeting. In a meeting there's usually a deadline and everyone knows they have to talk business and they have an agenda to guide them. Socializing is hard because people who don't know each other well have to find topics of mutual interest to talk about.

B 1 Look at these topics you might talk about when socializing with a foreign visitor you don't know very well. Tick the ones that look like GOOD topics to talk about, and put a cross by the ones which look like BAD topics to talk about. Write OK by the ones which might be OK when you get to know the person better. Add one more GOOD topic to the list.

art	food	money	sport
business	hobbies and interests	movies	television
current events	holidays	music	weather
family and children	local customs	racial tension	wine
fashion	local history	relationships	....

2 + Compare your choices. Explain the reasons for your choices if they're different from the other pair's. Then discuss these questions:

● Is it OK to talk business over a meal or drinks in your country? Or do people only talk business in the office?

● What is the topic you really hate to talk about most? What do you say if the topic comes up?

C 1 You can get an idea of someone's interests by asking them questions. But follow-up questions are even more important to keep the conversation going – as in the second version of Jim and Emma's conversation in A2.

What follow-up questions can you ask in these situations? Note down your ideas.

Question	Answer	Follow-up question
Did you read about . . . in the paper today?	Yes.	....
Is everything all right with your hotel?	Not really.	....
Have you been away on holiday this year?	Yes.	....
Have you seen any good movies lately?	Yes.	....
What kind of music do you like?	Classical.	....
What do you like to do in your spare time?	I like to read.	....
Will you have any time to see the city?	Yes.	....

2  Listen to the recording and compare your follow-up questions with the model versions.

> *Yes/No* questions are less productive when socializing than *Wh–* questions. *What kind of movies do you like?* is more likely to lead to a long, interesting answer than *Do you like movies?*
> The most useful questions of all when socializing are:
> . . . *What about you?* and . . . *What do you think?* because they encourage the other person to speak.

D 1 If possible, work with someone you don't usually work with. One of you should look at **File 15** on page 123, the other at **File 46** on page 135.

2 + Compare your experiences of socializing with business visitors. Discuss these questions:

● What did you enjoy about socializing?

● What tips or advice can you give on socializing with different nationalities?

● If you're not very good at small talk, how can you improve?

"I love a scary film."

www.CartoonStock.com

31 Would you like to join me for dinner?

Deciding where to eat • Table manners in different countries

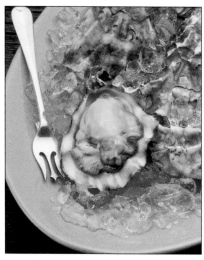

A **1** 👥 **Look at the photos and discuss these questions:**

- Where do you think the photos were taken?
- What is your favourite restaurant? Why?
- Would you take a business associate there? If not, where would you take him or her?
- Which of these factors influence your choice of a restaurant to take a business associate to?
  ambience • location • view • food • quality of service • value for money
- Which are the two most important factors?

2 🔊 👥 **Look at these restaurant descriptions and listen to Hans, the host, and Astrid deciding which to go to. Which one did they choose? Which one would you choose?**

Golden Dragon

Chinese Restaurant

In the heart of the old city
Outdoor terrace open in good weather
Finest Cantonese and Szechuan cooking
Dine with us in an elegant, relaxing
atmosphere and enjoy the finest dishes.
Mr and Mrs Chan and their family promise
you a friendly welcome and fine food.

Le Bistro

Opposite the rail station.
Authentic French cuisine.
Enjoy an intimate candlelit dinner.
Our meat is free-range and our
vegetables are organic.
Menus change daily.
We always offer a fish of the day
and a vegetarian alternative.

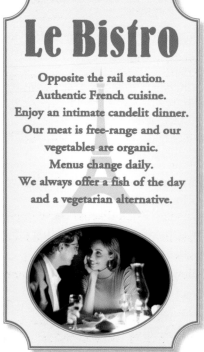

Trattoria Da Lorenzo

Overlooking the lake,
15 minutes from centre
Pizzas cooked in a wood-fired oven
Fresh locally-caught seafood is our
speciality
Home made pasta
Live music every evening from 8pm

B   **1**   🔊 **Listen to the conversation again and tick the phrases that the speakers used.**

Host		Guest	
Where would you like to eat?	☐	*Where do you recommend?*	☐
Well, the Golden Dragon is very nice.	☐	*What kind of food do they have there?*	☐
Lorenzo's is a nice place because . . .	☐	*I think I prefer the sound of the other place.*	☐
Their speciality is . . .	☐	*Do they have local specialities?*	☐

2 👥 **Think of four local specialities which you would recommend to a foreign visitor to your country. Write their names on a piece of paper as a sort of menu.**

Decide together how to describe the dishes in English, then join a different partner.

3 👥 **Work with a different partner. Take turns to play the roles of foreign guest and host.**

Host: Recommend the local specialities on your list.

Guest: Ask your host to guide your choices of what to eat.

C   **1**   👥 **Read this information about eating habits and good table manners in different countries. Can you guess the missing words?**

1 Japanese people have a clean _____ with them for drying hands and to use as a napkin at table – never for blowing the nose. All Japanese carry tissues.

2 In **Korea**, when drinking wait for someone to pour your drink, don't pour your own. Don't pour a drink into a glass unless it's _____ . If someone holds the bottle over your glass, it's a signal to drink up so that they can fill it. When holding your glass to be filled, use both hands.
   Make sure you're wearing nice _____ if you go to a Korean restaurant, because you may have to remove your shoes.

3 In **Taiwan**, it's bad luck to leave your chopsticks sticking vertically out of your bowl.
Don't _____ your chopsticks at people.

4 When eating **Thai** food, use your spoon in your _____ hand to pick up food and your fork to push it on in your _____ hand.

5 In **Spain**, dinner is eaten quite _____ – not until 9 or 10pm.
   It's quite normal for people to share starters.
   People often hold a _____ in the right hand and a piece of bread in the other.

6 In **Germany**, it's good manners for a man to enter a restaurant _____ a woman, and lead the way to a table.
   Glasses and cups aren't refilled _____ the guest has finished the contents.
   It's _____ manners to place your hand in your lap while eating.

7 In **Italy**, if you're invited out to dinner, offer to pay at the end, but allow your _____ to insist on paying.

8 Polish people say 'Thank you' at the end of a meal (thanking the others for their _____).

9 Russian people don't expect to eat at any particular time. You may be very _____ by the time anyone suggests going to a restaurant.

10 In _____ , if you're having steak, cut up some of it into bite-size pieces, then put down the knife and hold the fork in your right hand to move the food to your mouth. Use your _____ (held in your right hand) to cut vegetables and fish.

2 👥👥 **Compare your answers. Then discuss these questions:**

● How would people react in your country if you did some of the things in the text?

● What are some examples of good table manners in your country?

● What are some examples of bad table manners in your country? How do people react to them?

Travellers often like to try the food and drink of the region, rather than stick to familiar inter-national food. If possible, before you book a table, ask your visitors what kind of food they like to eat.

32 How do I get there?

Explaining routes • Suggesting free time activities

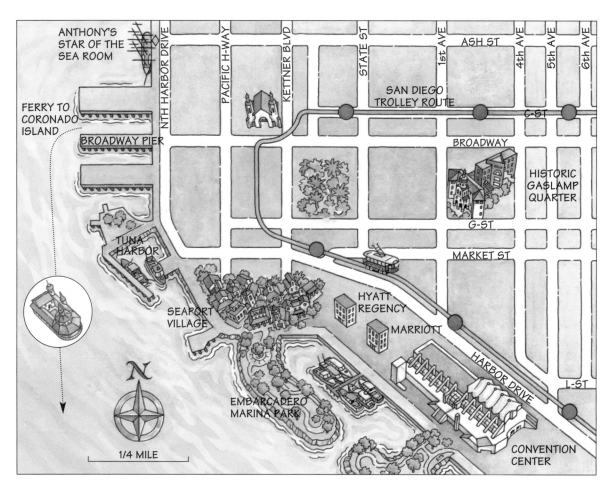

A 1 👥 **Find these places on the street map:**

Anthony's Star of the Sea Room   Broadway Pier   Convention Center   Harbor Drive
Historic Gaslamp Quarter   Hyatt Regency Hotel   Hotel del Coronado
San Diego Trolley route   Seaport Village

2 🔊 **Listen to local people giving directions to Leo, a British visitor. Highlight the places where each conversation happens and draw the route Leo takes.**

3 👥 **Take turns to play the role of visitor and resident. Start at Anthony's Star of the Sea Room and go back over Leo's route in reverse, asking for directions at each place he stopped.**

Can you tell me how to get to . . . ?

Yes, go straight along this street and it's on the right.

It's three blocks north of . . .

It's just around the corner from . . .

It's right next door to . . .

It's just opposite . . .

You go past . . .

The quickest/easiest way is to . . .

B 1 Decide how you would answer these questions about your town or city, which a visitor might ask you:

What are normal business hours?   When are the department stores open?

What time do people usually have lunch and dinner?   When are the banks open?

When is the Art Museum open?   Where can I buy some good local wine to take home?

2 Suppose a foreign visitor has a free afternoon, evening or Sunday in your town or city. What places would you recommend visiting? Fill this table with as many ideas as you can. Leave gaps if you can't think of anywhere.

	Afternoon	Evening	Sunday
cultural			
sporting			
sightseeing			
shopping			
nature			
historical			
where to see local people having fun			
somewhere out of town to go to			
a nice walk			
a good meal			

3 + Compare your lists. Explain your choices, if they're different. Fill any gaps with more ideas.

4 One of you should look at File 24 on page 127, the other at File 58 on page 140. You're going to play the roles of a guest in your city and the host. Begin your conversation like this:

I've got a bit of free time now. Can you recommend somewhere I could go?
Yes, very much!

Can you tell me where it is?

Do you like paintings?
Then I recommend the Art Museum. It's certainly worth visiting.
I'll show you on this street plan . . .

33 Do you have a room available?

Arranging hotel accommodation • Staying in a business hotel

Mr Wong

Mme Duval

Mr Stein

A **1** 👥 **Look at the photo and decide what the guests are saying to the receptionists.**

- Mr Wong has just arrived. He has a reservation. What does he say to the receptionist?
- Mme Duval has been in the hotel for three days. She wants to stay an extra night. What does she say?
- Mr Stein is leaving tomorrow at 5 am. What does he say?

2 🔊 **Listen to what the guests actually said. Write** W, D **or** S **to show who said what.**

.... *Can I check out and pay my bill in the morning?*

.... *Could I settle my bill this evening?*

.... *Could you book me a taxi to the airport, please?*

.... *Do you have a non-smoking room?*

.... *Do you have a room free?*

.... *Do you have a room with a balcony?*

.... *Good evening, my name's . . . . I have a room booked for tonight.*

.... *I don't mind moving to a different room if necessary.*

.... *I'd like a room that doesn't overlook the street, please.*

.... *I would like to extend my stay for another night.*

.... *I'm going to pay by Visa. Here's my card.*

3 👥👥 **Compare your experiences of hotels and discuss these questions:**

- Does your company use the same hotel to put up business visitors – and if so, why?
- Have you stayed in hotels while on business? What were they like? Which was the best and which was the worst – and why?
- What kind of facilities do you expect in a business hotel, but not in a holiday hotel?

Staff in a hotel are trained to deal with people who don't speak their language, so visitors to your country will probably have no difficulties in their hotel. But you may need to make sure they get the best treatment by talking to the staff there. If you always use the same hotel, this will probably make things easier – and they'll probably give you a special price for rooms.

B 1 **Listen to these phrases which you can use during your stay at a hotel. Practise saying them.**

asking for information	*What time is breakfast served in the morning?*
	Can I leave my case here till later today?
	How much will it cost if I want to . . . ?
requesting action	*Can I reserve a table for dinner for four people?*
	Could you call me a taxi, please?
	I'd like an alarm call at 6.30, please.
dealing with problems	*The . . . in my room doesn't seem to work.*
	Is there someone who can fix the . . . in my room?
	I couldn't sleep last night – the people in the room next to mine were making a lot of noise.
	I don't think these charges are right – can you explain them, please?

2 One of you should look at File 25 on page 127, the other at File 59 on page 140. You'll be playing the roles of guest and hotel receptionist.

C 1 Your US distributor, Mary Rossi, is visiting your factory with her assistant Dan Johnson. She has sent you this e-mail:

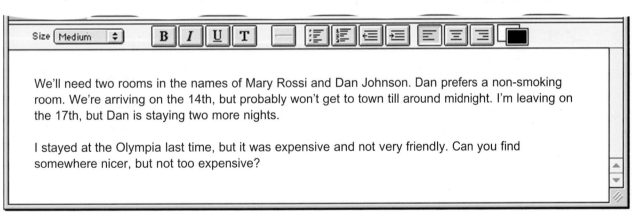

Size [Medium ▼]   **B** *I* <u>U</u> **T**

We'll need two rooms in the names of Mary Rossi and Dan Johnson. Dan prefers a non-smoking room. We're arriving on the 14th, but probably won't get to town till around midnight. I'm leaving on the 17th, but Dan is staying two more nights.

I stayed at the Olympia last time, but it was expensive and not very friendly. Can you find somewhere nicer, but not too expensive?

Your firm will pay her hotel expenses during her stay in your town.
Write an e-mail to the Phoenix Hotel to book rooms.

2 Look at File 26 on page 127. Then follow the directions from there.

3 Discuss these questions:
- What kinds of things can go wrong with hotel bookings?
- What kinds of things can go wrong while you're staying at a hotel?
- What has been your own worst experience in a hotel?
- What has been your own most pleasant experience in a hotel?

34 When things go wrong . . .

Dealing with travel and accommodation problems • Advising people what to do

A 1 👥 **Look at the photos and discuss these questions:**
- What has happened to the people in the photos?
- What do you think they should do?

2 🔊 👥 **Listen to four visitors phoning their host to ask for help. Look at the alternatives and decide what each person's problem is. What do you think they should do?**

1	Mr Allen's problem:	He has missed his flight.
		His flight is overbooked and he can't get a seat.
2	Ms Barnes's problem:	She has lost her credit card.
		The hotel won't accept her credit card.
3	Mr Schranz's problem:	He left his suitcase in a taxi.
		Someone has taken his suitcase by mistake.
4	Ms Davis's problem:	Her traveller's cheques have been stolen.
		She forgot to bring any traveller's cheques with her.
5	Mr Allen's other problem:	He has gone to the wrong hotel.
		The hotel is full.

3 🔊 👥 **Listen to the advice their host gave or the action he took. Do you agree with him?**

If you're travelling (alone) on business, you may have to sort out your own problems. The hotel concierge or airline staff may be able to help you. Or you may have to contact your hosts. So make sure you have their home and mobile phone numbers, not only their office numbers. Most problems seem to happen outside office hours.

B **1**  Imagine that your guest has these problems. Decide what he/she should do in each situation. What advice would you give to your guest?

> I think you should . . .   It might be a good idea to . . .
> The only thing to do is . . .   The best thing to do is . . .

1   Your guest has arrived at the airport on Sunday afternoon after a long flight. The passport officer refuses to admit her because her passport expires in five months' time. She phones you at home. What do you say to your guest?

2   Your guest's flight is delayed and it doesn't get in till 2 am. There are no taxis and no buses. What do you say to your guest?

3   Your guest is about to fly to an island for important business meetings on Tuesday but the weather forecast says that a typhoon is headed that way and will be there on Wednesday, if not earlier. All flights may be grounded for several days during the typhoon. Should he cancel the trip? Or try to get in and out before the typhoon? What do you advise?

4   You and your guest are booked on an internal flight to a provincial capital. When you get to the airport your guest tells you that the flight is on an airline she doesn't trust in a very old plane. She's afraid it will crash. What do you say to your guest?

5   You've been out celebrating with your guest. He's leaving the country first thing tomorrow morning. You walk him back to his hotel. Then he discovers that his pocket has been picked – he no longer has his passport, tickets or money. What do you say to your guest?

6   You are seeing your guest off at the airport. She is checking in for her flight and the ticket clerk points out that her ticket is dated yesterday. Today's flight is full. What do you say to your guest?

2 ▪ + ▪ Compare your solutions.

C **1** ▪ What advice would you give to a guest about avoiding problems in your town or city? Add three DOS and four DON'TS to this list:

> DO lock your hotel room door
>   go by taxi at night
>   reconfirm your flight

> DON'T carry a lot of cash with you
>   walk alone in the city centre
>   after midnight

2 ▪ Compare your lists. Then discuss these questions:
- What is the most valuable piece of advice you've come up with?
- What problems have you had when travelling (on business or for pleasure)?
- What do/would you enjoy and not enjoy about travelling on business?

 If your guest has a problem, he/she may ask you to help because you understand the way things work in your country and who to ask for specialist help. For example, if your guest's car breaks down, you are more likely to know a good local mechanic than he/she is.

(35) About the company

Explaining the history and structure of a company

(A) **1** 👥 **Look at the photos and discuss these questions:**
- What kind of company is easyJet?
- What do you already know about easyJet and easyEverything?

2 🔊 **Toby Nicol works for easyJet. Listen to him talking about the history of the airline and fill the blanks.**

easyJet

founded in _____ by Stelios Haji-Ioannou
no _____ low _____ airline
_____ aircraft flying on _____ routes, all within _____
floated on the stock market in _____ , value almost £ _____ million

Other easyGroup companies:

easyEverything – a chain of _____ cafés. The first one opened in London in _____ .
Now there are many more, including the world's largest in Times Square, _____ .

easyRentacar – the world's first _____ -only car rental company. Costs are kept down by
only using one _____ of car.

easyValue.com – a website with 'robot' _____ that searches for the best _____ on
different companies' websites.

3 🔊 **Now listen to Toby talking about the structure of easyJet. Fill the blanks in the summary.**

Company structure:

_____ (Stelios Haji-Ioannou)
Chief _____
Board of _____
Management _____

easyJet has a very _____ management structure. They have a _____ office system,
which makes it easy to communicate _____ and externally. The company is based in
easyLand, a bright _____ converted shed at Luton Airport. The offices are
open- _____ , everyone dresses _____ , there are no _____ , no _____
offices. easyJet is all about taking frills and _____ out of the business in order to
minimize _____ . This is how they can continue to offer _____ fares to customers.

4 👥👥👥👥 Discuss these questions:

● Would you like to work for one of the easyGroup companies? Why (not)?
● How is the company structure different from companies you know or have worked for?

5 👥👥👥👥 Write down the names of two well-known companies in your city or region. Discuss what you know about each company's activities:

● Where do they operate? How important are they?
● If you could choose, which would you like to work for? Why?

B **1** 👥👥 Which of these words can you use to talk about your own company and your own office? (Or a company you know, or have worked for.) Add any extra words you need to the lists.

Types of company	Divisions	Employees
firm	parent company	head of department
(USA) corporation	sister company	director
multinational	division	(USA) CEO (chief executive officer)
conglomerate	branch	(GB) MD (managing director)
family business	(GB) head office/(USA) home office	supervisor
organization	department	assistant
	section	team leader
	office	staff

2 👥👥 Look at this extract from an organizational chart. Match the answers on the right below to the questions on the left.

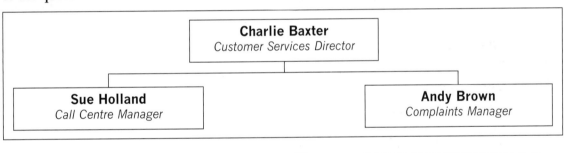

	Charlie Baxter *Customer Services Director*	
Sue Holland *Call Centre Manager*		**Andy Brown** *Complaints Manager*

1	What is Andy Brown's job?	a	Andy Brown
2	Which department is Andy Brown in charge of?	b	Charlie Baxter
3	Which department is Sue Holland responsible for?	c	He's the Complaints Manager.
4	Which managers are under Charlie Baxter?	d	She's the Call Centre Manager.
5	Who does Sue Holland report to?	e	Sue Holland and Andy Brown
6	Who is responsible for complaints?	f	The Call Centre
7	Who is Sue Holland?	g	The Complaints Department

3 👥👥 One of you should look at File 23 on page 126, the other at File 57 on page 139. You'll be looking at another organizational chart.

4 👥👥👥👥 Discuss these questions about your present company (or a company you've worked for):

● Does the company have a clear structure (as in Perfect Products in Files 23 and 57)? Or do people work in teams?
● How has the organization changed since you've worked there?
● What changes do you think there will be/should be in future?

36 Let me demonstrate . . .

Explaining what to do • Showing people how to do things

A Swatch Musicall

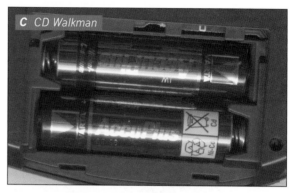

C CD Walkman

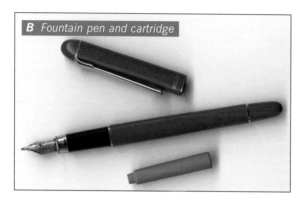

B Fountain pen and cartridge

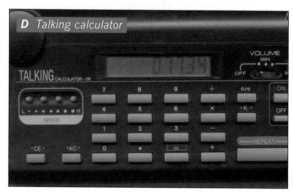

D Talking calculator

A **1** 🔊 Listen to four operations being explained. Match the photos above to the clips you hear.

2 🔊 Listen again. Note down the most important point each speaker made.

1		3	
2		4	

3 👥 Compare your answers. Which was the easiest explanation to follow? Why was it easier?

B **1** 🔊 👥 Listen to another demonstration. Tick the phrases that the speakers used:

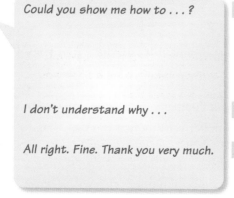

Could you show me how to . . . ? ☐

I don't understand why . . . ☐

All right. Fine. Thank you very much. ☐

OK, let me show you. Just watch what I do. ☐
First of all . . . ☐
The next thing you have to do is . . . ☐
Whatever you do, don't . . . ☐
Be very careful not to . . . ☐
Well, the reason why you have to do that is . . . ☐
OK so far? ☐
So that's about it. Any questions? ☐
OK now you try . I'll watch and help if I need to. ☐

2 👥 Go through the same operation step by step. Take turns to be the 'expert'.

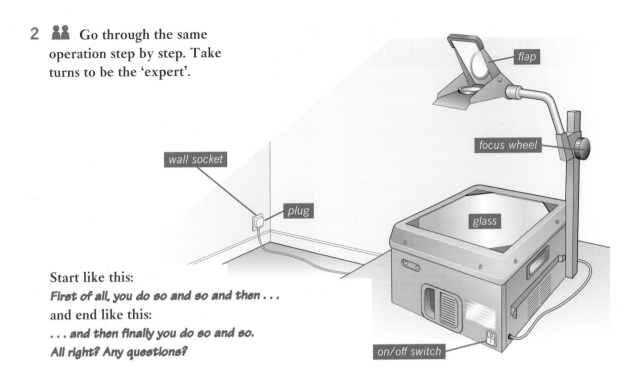

Start like this:
First of all, you do so and so and then . . .
and end like this:
. . . and then finally you do so and so.
All right? Any questions?

3 👥 + 👥 Here are some operations which are pretty easy – once you know how. But not so easy to learn the first time. Pick ONE operation. Each pair should pick a DIFFERENT one.
- how to store a new number on a mobile phone
- how to use a MiniDisc or MP3 player
- how to download something from the Internet
- how to unblock a paper jam on a printer or photocopier
- how to programme radio stations on a car radio
- how to get cash from an ATM

4 👥 Work out how to perform your operation. Then join a student from the other pair.

5 👥 Explain to your new partner how to perform your operation. Pretend not to know while your partner demonstrates and then helps you.

C **1** 👥 One of you should look at File 27 on page 128, the other at File 61 on page 141. You'll be explaining how to perform two more operations.

2 👥👥 Discuss these questions:
- In your work, what kinds of operations do/will you have to explain to people?
- What do you find most difficult when people are explaining something to you?
- Some people are better at explaining than others. What do they do that makes them good?

⭐ If you're demonstrating something and the other person is watching you closely, you don't need to know what all the components are called. You can say: *'Open this'* instead of *'Open this flap'*, and *'Press this'* instead of *'Press this button'*.

37 How does it work?

Describing processes and procedures

A 1  Joost Meijerink is General Manager of Flexifoil. His company designs high-tech kites: for normal kite-flying and for kite-surfing (see photo). He describes the process from design to distribution. As you listen for the first time, note down your answers to these questions:

1 What are computers used for?
2 How long does the whole process take?

2 Listen again and fill the blanks in this flow diagram.

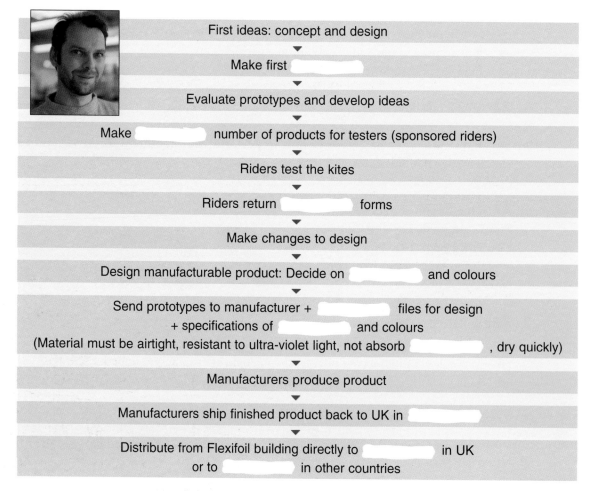

First ideas: concept and design
▼
Make first ⬚
▼
Evaluate prototypes and develop ideas
▼
Make ⬚ number of products for testers (sponsored riders)
▼
Riders test the kites
▼
Riders return ⬚ forms
▼
Make changes to design
▼
Design manufacturable product: Decide on ⬚ and colours
▼
Send prototypes to manufacturer + ⬚ files for design
+ specifications of ⬚ and colours
(Material must be airtight, resistant to ultra-violet light, not absorb ⬚ , dry quickly)
▼
Manufacturers produce product
▼
Manufacturers ship finished product back to UK in ⬚
▼
Distribute from Flexifoil building directly to ⬚ in UK
or to ⬚ in other countries

3 Compare your answers. Then discuss these questions:

- Which processes and procedures can you show someone on a tour of your company?
- Which of your company's procedures and processes does a client or new employee need to know about?

> Every aspect of business involves procedures, which can be broken down into steps or stages. Stage 2 can't begin until Stage 1 is finished . . . and so on. There may be simultaneous stages, done by different people, which all have to be done before the next stage can be started.

B **1**  Make notes on the procedure of writing and sending an e-mail. Draw a flow chart.

2 Listen to an explanation of the procedure of sending an e-mail. Then discuss these questions:

- Did you include the same steps as the speaker did?
- Did the speaker leave any steps out?
- How is the procedure you follow different from the one the speaker explained?

3 Take turns to explain the procedure to each other, playing the roles of 'new employee' and 'supervisor'.

> If you want to send an e-mail, choose the e-mail program on your computer.
>
> First of all, click 'New Message'.   After that . . .
>
> Once you've done that . . .   So then . . .
>
> Next . . .   Finally . . .

C **1** What do you know about how a calculator works? Tell each other what you know.

2 One of you should look at **File 28** on page 128, the other at **File 62** on page 141. You'll find out more information to share with your partner.

> You may have to explain a procedure or process to a new colleague or to a new client. If you can't actually show the person (by demonstrating the procedure or taking them on a tour of the factory), you'll probably need pictures or diagrams. These need to be prepared in advance.

38 Features and benefits!

Marketing and advertising • Sales talk

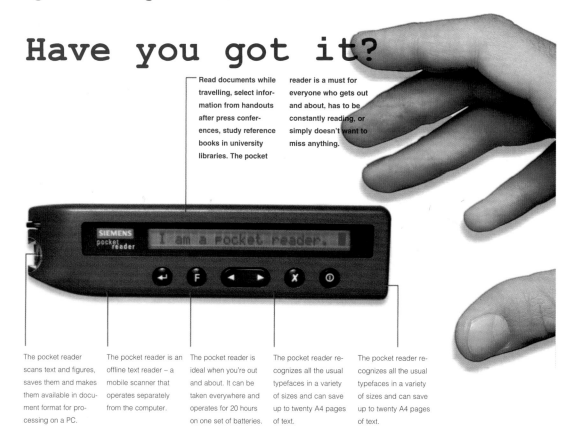

Have you got it?

Read documents while travelling, select information from handouts after press conferences, study reference books in university libraries. The pocket reader is a must for everyone who gets out and about, has to be constantly reading, or simply doesn't want to miss anything.

I am a pocket reader.

The pocket reader scans text and figures, saves them and makes them available in document format for processing on a PC.

The pocket reader is an offline text reader – a mobile scanner that operates separately from the computer.

The pocket reader is ideal when you're out and about. It can be taken everywhere and operates for 20 hours on one set of batteries.

The pocket reader recognizes all the usual typefaces in a variety of sizes and can save up to twenty A4 pages of text.

The pocket reader recognizes all the usual typefaces in a variety of sizes and can save up to twenty A4 pages of text.

A 1 Look at the product description and discuss these questions:

- Why might people buy the product? How many reasons can you think of?
- Who are the target customers for the product?
- Are you a target customer? Would you consider buying the product? Why/Why not?
- What questions would you ask a salesperson about the product?

You've got it:
The world's first <u>offline</u> text reader.

2 Match the questions on the left to the answers on the right:

Marketing and advertising

1 What are the product's **features**?
2 What are the product's **benefits**?
3 What is the product's **USP** ('Unique Selling Proposition')?

a This is what makes it different from competing products.
b This is how buying the product will bring an advantage to the person who buys it.
c This is what the product looks like and what it does.

3 Look again at the ad and discuss these questions:
- What are the features of the product?
- What seem to be the benefits of the product?
- What seems to be the USP of the product?

It's not just consumers who buy goods:

Several suppliers sell components and/or raw materials to a manufacturer . . .

The manufacturer sells to several wholesalers (or agents) . . .

They sell to many retailers . . .

And, hopefully, they sell to even more consumers (end-users).

Every company is involved in selling (and buying) – and every contact with another company may be a sales opportunity.

Just like goods, services are products which are bought and sold.

B **1** **Listen to Maria and Peter talking to two customers. Note down which features and benefits of the Pocket Reader they mention.**

	Maria	Peter
features		
benefits		
USP		

2 **Discuss these questions:**

- How are the benefits to the wholesaler or retailer different from the benefits to the end-user (consumer)?
- What questions would the wholesaler or retailer ask, which the end-users wouldn't?

C **1** **Two of you should look at File 29 on page 129, the other two at File 68 on page 144. You'll find out about two more products which you'll have to 'sell'.**

2 **Join a different partner. Take turns to play the roles of supplier and customer. Here are some phrases you can use when you tell your customer about your product:**

arouse interest	Have you seen/tried this product before?
	How much do you already know about it?
features	Let me give you some information about this product . . .
benefits	If you buy this product, you . . .
USP	The best thing about this product is . . .
encourage action	Would you like to place an order?

(When you play the role of customer, show interest in the product!)

D

Preparation Before Unit 39, cut out a couple of your favourite advertisements from magazines or newspapers. Bring them to class with you for the lesson. Also read the advice on giving a presentation on page 82.

39 Giving presentations

Preparing and giving a presentation

A

1 👥 **Look at the photo and think of presentations you've attended. Brainstorm these ideas:**

- What kept you interested – and why did you lose interest for a while?
- What are the features of a really good presentation?

2 👥 **Read this advice. There are** FOUR **deliberate mistakes – can you find them?**

If you're going to give a presentation, remember the Three Ps:

Before . . .

Plan what you're going to say:

What are your 3 or 4 *key points*?

Find out about your *audience*: Who are they? How many of them will there be?

Research the topic (in-house material, websites, reports, ideas from colleagues).

Prepare your talk:

Write the presentation out in full. Then extract the main points and put them on *index cards*. Use large clear writing (or print) so that you can read your notes easily. Number the cards clearly (so that if you drop them, you can't rearrange them easily).

Are you going to use *visual aids*: OHP transparencies, computer graphics, handouts, flipchart? If so, prepare everything in advance. Use big print for things the audience will have to read on a screen.

Anticipate the *questions* you may be asked. Prepare answers to them.

End on a strong, positive note. Use a memorable phrase as you finish.

Practise giving your talk into a tape recorder or in front of a window.

Find a *friend* to be your 'audience' – he/she can ask you questions and give you feedback at the end.

Practise using the *visual aids*.

Practise *losing* your place in your notes, and finding it again.

Test the equipment at the venue after the audience arrive. Does everything work properly?

Can people at the back read what's on the *screen*? If you dim the lights or close the blinds, is it too dark for everyone to make notes or see the handouts? Do you need to use a *microphone*? Does it work?

During . . .

Speak *clearly* and not too fast. Behave naturally.

Involve your audience – look at them, talk to them, keep eye contact, ask them questions.

After . . .

Make sure there's enough time for *questions* before your presentation.

3 👥 **Think of two more tips for good presentations and write them down.**

B 1 🔊 👥 Listen to clips from two presentations: Alan is a poor presenter, Becky is quite good. Put a cross beside the advice Alan didn't follow and a tick beside the advice Becky did follow in A2. Did they follow your own tips?

2 🔊 👥 Listen to these phrases and practise saying them.

starting off	*Good morning, ladies and gentlemen.*
	Good morning, everyone.
'say what you're going to say'	*What I'm going to talk about is . . .*
	I'm going to tell you about . . .
structuring the talk	*Right, first of all . . . Finally . . .*
introducing your fellow-presenter	*Now I'd like to hand over to . . .*
	She's going to tell you about . . .
'say what you've said'	*So, what are the important points I've made? Well, first . . .*
	So, to summarize: . . .
at the end, ask for questions	*Thank you very much for listening. Now, do you have any questions?*
	If you have any questions, I'm pleased to answer them.
answering difficult questions	*I need to think about that one. Could we come back to it later?*
	I don't really know the answer to that. Could we discuss it later?

C 1 👥 Look at the ads you've both brought to class (see D on page 81). Decide which one is your favourite or the most effective.

Prepare a joint presentation on the ad, covering these aspects:

- What kind of customers is the ad directed at?
- What are the features of the product?   What are the benefits of the product?
- What is the product's 'unique selling proposition'?
- Why is the ad effective?   Why do you like it?

Each of you should talk for about the same amount of time. Decide who's going to say what – and when you're going to hand over.

2 👥 + 👥 Join another pair. Each pair gives their presentation. The others are the audience.

Presenters: Give your presentation. Ask for questions at the end.

Audience: Don't interrupt during the presentation (unless you are asked a question). While you're in the audience, note down a question to ask at the end.

3 👥👥 After all the presentations, give each other feedback and discuss these questions:

- What was good about each presentation?
- What would you have done differently if you'd had more time to prepare?
- What tips can you give each other for the next time you have to give a presentation?
- What kinds of presentations do/will you have to give in your real job?

The audience are not your enemy – they are on your side, they want to learn from you.

If someone asks a question in a quiet voice, repeat it to the whole audience. Then address your answer to the whole audience.

If you can't answer a question, maybe someone else in the audience can.

40 A great new product!

Product development • Giving a presentation

If you can come up with a great new product, patent it and sell it, you can make your fortune! But has someone else had the idea before you?

Serve drinks to your guests with this new doggy tray system.

No Desk?

Make notes on this ingenious arm-mounted notepad!

A 🏃🏃🏃🏃 Work in groups of three or four for each part of this section of the lesson.

1 Here's your chance to dream up a great new product! First, discuss these questions:

- What products does the world need, which aren't yet generally available?
- What products would you buy, if they existed?
- Are the products you thought of too expensive until the technology and production techniques have been developed? Or maybe the technology doesn't even exist yet?

2 Pick one of these products. (Imagine that they can be mass-produced and are not too expensive.) Or better still: invent your own product!

A voice-powered TV/VCR/hi-fi/DVD. You say 'Channel 4' and it changes the channel, or 'Louder' and it increases the volume – no need for a remote control.	A talking postcard – you speak your message into a built-in microphone, post it and the other person can hear your message through the built-in loudspeaker.
A solar-powered electric bike – it even works in cloudy weather.	A designer business suit that never creases, never needs cleaning and never wears out.
A pocket drinks cooler – it cools a can or bottle in 30 seconds.	A pill you can take to cure a cold instantly – just one tablet and your cold has gone.

3 Design your product and decide on its features: how does it work and what can it do? How much is it going to cost the end-user?

4 Design a magazine ad for the product.

5 Prepare a joint presentation of the product, which you will give to the buyers of a chain store who are thinking of stocking the product. Make sure each of you has a part to play.

B **1** **Whole class** Listen to each other's presentations and give your own.

2 Evaluate the other groups. You aren't allowed to vote for your own group.

Vote for the best ad.

Vote for the best product.

Vote for the best presentation.

"Really, Muriel, must we go through this every time I work late at the office?"

Grammar reference

Contents

Adverbs and word order

Different adverbs and adverb phrases may fit 'comfortably' in different places in a sentence: at the beginning, in the middle or at the end.

1 Some adverbs and adverb phrases can go in all three positions:

Recently, he was promoted.   He was recently promoted.   He was promoted recently.

Unexpectedly, he was promoted. He was unexpectedly promoted. He was promoted unexpectedly.

2 Some adverbs feel most comfortable **at the end**:

He was promoted by his boss.   He was promoted yesterday.

I'll phone you tomorrow.   Can you phone me in the afternoon?

3 These adverbs usually feel most comfortable in the **middle** position:

almost · always · certainly · completely · ever · frequently · hardly · hardly ever · nearly · never · obviously · often probably · rarely · seldom

They certainly promoted him.   He has never been promoted.

Notice where middle position adverbs are placed when there is a **modal verb** in the sentence:

He will certainly be promoted. ✓   He will be certainly promoted. ✗

He will never be promoted. ✓   He will be never promoted. ✗

4 An adverb is **not** normally placed between a verb and a direct object:

I like tennis very much. ✓   I like very much tennis. ✗

He drove the car very fast. ✓   He drove very fast the car. ✗

Articles and quantifiers

1 Most nouns are **countable**, for example:

car (we can talk about a car and some cars) · *bus · train · truck · taxi · component*

but some nouns are **uncountable** and take a singular verb, for example:

electricity · fuel · equipment · information · machinery · weather · advice · progress · news · stationery

We can't say: an information ✗ OR informations ✗

But we can say: some information OR any information

We can't say: a good news ✗ OR an equipment ✗

But we can say:

a piece of good news OR some good news OR any good news OR a piece of equipment

The news is good.   The weather was awful.

2 **Quantifiers** are words like *some, any, few, less, much* and *many*:

There's some printing paper on my desk, and there are some envelopes in the top drawer.

There isn't any printing paper left – and there aren't any envelopes either.

Is there any printing paper left? Are there any envelopes left?

Is there some printing paper left? Are there some envelopes too? (hopefully expecting the answer *Yes*)

Little, less, the least and *much* are only used with uncountable nouns and singular countable nouns.
Few, fewer, the fewest and *many* are only used with plural countable nouns:

There isn't much paper left.   There's very little paper left.

There aren't many envelopes left.   There are only a few envelopes left.

Alan has fewer days' holiday than he'd like to have.

Betty earns less money than she'd like to.

Dave has the fewest days' holiday and earns the least money.

3 *The* is used in these cases:

a Referring to things that are **unique** (in other words, only **one** of them exists):

The most popular summer sport in   Is Manchester United the best football team
  Britain is cricket.   in the UK?

The President of the United States   I'm worried about the future.

The sea is too rough to swim in. What time does the sun rise?

b When it's **obvious** which one you mean:

We're going to the canteen – you can join us there later.

You'll have to talk to the boss if you want a day off.

How many employees are there in the office?

I'll just check this on the computer.

c When we mean a **particular** person or thing:

The person who signed the letter is my assistant.

The shipment we sent on Friday should arrive on Monday.

I can't find the instruction manual for this machine.

d Oceans, seas and rivers:

the Atlantic, the Aegean, the Mediterranean, the Thames, the Rhine

e **Plural** mountain groups, island groups and countries:

the Andes, the Canary Islands, the Netherlands, the Philippines

f Hotels, cinemas, theatres, museums:

the Ritz, the Gaumont, the Playhouse, the National Gallery, the Tate Gallery

4 *A* or ***an*** is used in these cases:

a Referring to a **single** thing or person:

There's a bank opposite the cinema.

She's a colleague of Peter's.

A friend of mine is coming to visit.

It was quite an interesting story.

b **Professions** or jobs:

He's an accountant.

My father's a mechanic.

She's an engineer.

My mother's a teacher.

c **Generalisations**:

An accountant works in an office.

A company usually has a website.

A manager has to be a good leader.

An electric vehicle is pollution-free.

5 **Ø** – the 'zero article' – is used in these cases:

a **Generalisations** about plural ideas, people or things:

Acccountants work in offices.

Websites are an important marketing tool.

Dictionaries are useful.

Managers have to be good leaders.

Electric vehicles are pollution-free.

Factories are noisy places.

b Referring to concepts and ideas that are **uncountable**:

employment · freedom · knowledge · negligence · pollution · music · productivity · responsibility · tennis · watching television · swimming

Productivity has risen by 5%.

Swimming is a good way to keep fit.

c With these places, but only when they're used for their **main** purpose, rather than just for a visit or considered as buildings:

He went to school in England.	= he was educated
You mustn't smoke in class.	= during lessons
We go to church every Sunday.	= to worship
She's in hospital.	= for treatment
He's going to university.	= to study

BUT:

She drove to the school to pick up her son, then to the university to pick up her daughter.

d Continents, countries, states:

Europe Britain Holland France California Texas

BUT:

the United Kingdom the Netherlands the Philippines

e Languages:

English Dutch Korean Japanese Greek

f Mountains and lakes:

Mount Fuji Lake Geneva Ben Nevis Lake Superior

g Streets, roads and squares:

Oxford Street London Road Fifth Avenue Trafalgar Square

h Parks, stations and most public buildings:

Central Park Victoria Station Gatwick Airport Buckingham Palace Windsor Castle

BUT:

the Acropolis the Statue of Liberty the Eiffel Tower the Empire State Building

Comparing and contrasting

Office workers			
	Average working hours per week	**Average annual weeks' vacation**	**Annual number of public holidays**
UK	41	4	8
USA	40	2	10
France	35	5	12
Germany	37	6	14
Japan	40	2	12
Mexico	42	2	13

These examples show the principal uses of comparatives and superlatives. Pay particular attention to the way in which **similar** ideas can be expressed in **different** ways.

According to the chart:

Office workers in Mexico work longer hours than the other nationalities in the chart.
= Mexican employees work the longest hours of all.

There's not much difference between the number of hours the French and the Germans work.
= The French and the Germans work a similar number of hours.

British employees spend less time on vacation than the Germans.
= British employees don't spend as much time on holiday as the Germans.

British people have twice as many weeks' vacation as the Americans.
= Americans have half as many weeks' vacation as the British.

The French work much shorter hours than the Americans.
= The French work far fewer hours than the Americans.

The Germans have more public holidays than any of the other people in the chart.
= The Germans have the greatest number of public holidays.
= Nobody has as many public holidays as the Germans.

There are the same number of public holidays in Japan as in France.
= Japan and France have the same number of public holidays.

There are not as many public holidays in the UK as in Mexico.
= There are fewer public holidays in the UK than in Mexico.

The future

1   For **predictions** and **general** statements about the future, *will* or *will be doing* or *will have done* are used:

In the future, will business people still send letters by post?
I expect it will rain tomorrow.
By the end of this year we'll have sold 10,000 units.
While I'm working, my brother will be enjoying himself on holiday.
I'm sure the financial situation will have improved by the end of the week.
This time next year we'll be in our new offices – if everything goes according to plan.

Remember that *will* and *'ll* are not normally used in a clause following a **time conjunction**:

when · if · until · before · after · while · by the time

If you do all your work today, you'll be able to take it easy tomorrow.

We need to make copies before the meeting begins.

After the meeting has finished, we're going to have dinner together.

If you use a highlighter, you'll find it easier to remember the new words.

The short form *'ll* is normally only used after pronouns:

I'll send you a copy.   It'll be quicker to send it by UPS.

but in writing, or for emphasis, the full form *will* is often used:

I will send you a copy.   It will be quicker to send it by UPS.

2   For **inevitable** future events that we can 'see coming', *going to* is used:

One day there's going to be a terrible accident if we don't improve safety procedures.

My wife's going to have a baby.

The boss is going to be really angry when he reads the report.

3   For **intentions**, *going to* is used:

I'm going to leave now.

We're going to send all our customers the new catalogue.

I'm going to write the report later, when I've got more time.

4   For **arrangements**, the **present continuous** is used:

I'm seeing the human resources people at 2:30.

We're sending our customers the catalogue and a price list.

She's meeting two of our clients this afternoon.

I can't meet you this evening because I'm working late.

5   For **fixed events** on a timetable or calendar, the **present simple** is used:

The Americans celebrate Independence Day on July 4.

The plane from London lands at 09:30.

6   For **promises**, **suggestions** and **offers**, *will* is used:

I'll pay for lunch if you help me with this report.

I'll help you tomorrow.

Give me your suitcase and I'll put it in the boot of the car for you.

Normally, *shall* is only used when making an offer or a suggestion:

Shall I help you? ✓   Will I help you? ✗

Shall we take a break now? ✓   Will we take a break now? ✗

and **not** in these cases:

He shan't arrive on time. ✗   He won't arrive on time. ✓

They shall be late. ✗   They'll (will) be late. ✓

7   In most of the examples in 1–5, *going to* could be used instead of *will* or a **present tense**:

- In conversations and informal writing, *going to* is more common than *will*.
- In formal writing, *will* is more often used.

A rule of thumb for conversation is:

If in doubt, use *going to* – except if you're making a promise, offer or suggestion (when *going to* may sound like a threat).

If . . . sentences (Conditionals)

If . . . sentences are used to describe or imagine the consequences of events. There are four basic types of conditional sentences:

0   *If* + **present**, followed by the **present**, is used to express the consequences of events that are certain to happen – often general or scientific truths:

  If water is heated to 100°, it boils.
  If people don't have a healthy diet, they become ill.

1   *If* + **present**, followed by *will*, is used to imagine the **consequences** of events that are **likely to happen**, or to describe the consequences of events that **always happen**:

  If our flight lands on time, we'll arrive in time for lunch.
  If you place your order before December, you'll get a 10% discount.
  If you intend to go to the USA, you'll have to get a visa.
  If you've paid by credit card, you'll receive the shipment tomorrow.

  Unless (= *except if*) and *in case* can also be used in this type of conditional sentence:

  I won't open the letters unless you want me to.
  You won't be able to work the machine unless you've read the instructions.
  I'll get some money in case I have to pay for lunch.
  I'll take a street map with me in case I get lost.

2   *If* + **past**, followed by *would*, is used when we want to imagine the **consequences** of events that are **unlikely to happen** or events that **can't possibly happen**:

  What would you do if you could go anywhere in the world?
  — If I had enough money, I'd go to Brazil.
  If you had £10,000 to spend, where would you spend your holiday?
  If I was (or were) a millionaire, I wouldn't need to work.

  In some situations, we can use either type, depending on what we mean exactly:

  I would go the USA if I had enough money.   (. . . but I haven't got enough.)
  I'll go to the USA if I manage to save up enough money. (more optimistic)
  If I passed my driving test first time, I'd think about   (I probably have no immediate
    buying a car.   plans to take my test.)
  If I pass my driving test first time, I'll think about buying a car. (I'm probably taking it soon.)

  If I were you is often used for giving advice:

  If you were me, what would you do in this situation?
  — If I were you, I'd stay at home.

3   *If* + **past perfect**, followed by *would have*, is used when we want to imagine the opposite of **past** events:

  If I had known about the delay, I wouldn't have got to the airport so early.
  If there hadn't been a mix-up with our booking, we'd have had a room with a view.
  If you had reminded me to confirm the booking, I'd have written a letter.

  Remember that *'d* is the short form of both *had* and *would*:

  If he'd (he had) reminded me, I'd have (I would have) arrived on time.
  If I'd had (I had had) more time, I'd have (I would have) finished my work.

–ing and to __

The –*ing* form can be a present participle (as part of a verb or as an adjective) or it can be the noun form of a verb ('a gerund'):

verb	adjective	noun
I'm waiting for a phone call.	a marketing manager	Marketing is important in every company.
Are you feeling OK?	a typing error	Typing accurately is difficult.

1   –*ing* is used as the **subject** or **object** of a verb:

Giving a presentation is difficult.   Flying first class is expensive.
Working abroad is interesting.   Sitting in front of a computer all day is bad for your eyes.
I don't like flying   He enjoys playing tennis.

2   –*ing* is used after **prepositions**:

Is anyone interested in joining me?   I'm looking forward to going away on holiday.
I can't get used to working 9 to 5 every day.   She was fired after losing her temper.

3   Most **adjectives** are followed by *to* __ (the infinitive). For example:

pleased · glad · surprised · disappointed · relieved · shocked · interesting · kind · hard · essential · difficult · easy

I am pleased to meet you.   It was kind of you to invite me.
We were surprised to get a bill for £45 million.   It was easier to do than I had expected.
We were sorry to hear your bad news.   He was afraid to answer the phone.

BUT many common adjectives are followed by a **preposition + –*ing*** (see 2 above). For example:

afraid of · interested in · sorry about · good at · capable of · famous for · fond of

She's afraid of flying.   They're capable of doing better work than that.
We're interested in stocking your product.   They're very good at dealing with problems.

4   *to* __ is also used in the structures: *too . . . to* __ and *. . . enough to* __ *. . .*

We arrived early enough to get a seat.   This coffee is too hot to drink.
The desk is too heavy for me to lift.   This machine isn't reliable enough for us to buy.

5   Some **verbs** are usually followed by –*ing*:

avoid · can't help · delay · dislike · don't mind · enjoy · finish · give up · go on · practise · stop

I've finished writing my report.   I'm trying to give up smoking.
I couldn't help laughing when he fell over.   Please stop making that noise, it's driving me mad!

6   Some **verbs** are usually followed by *to* __:

afford · agree · choose · decide · expect · forget · hope · learn · manage · mean · need · offer · pretend · promise · refuse · remember · try · want · would like

allow someone · encourage someone · help someone · persuade someone · recommend someone · teach someone · train someone

They promised to invite me to lunch.   He didn't mean to be rude to our best client.
I can't afford to stay at the Ritz.   We decided to meet for a drink after work.
Did you remember to send the samples?   She taught him to use the machine.

7   Some **verbs** are followed by –*ing* or by *to* __ with no real difference in meaning.

begin · continue · intend · hate · like · love · prefer · propose · start

She began to eat/eating her meal.   I love to eat/eating Chinese food.
I don't like eating/to eat alone in restaurants.   Which dessert do you intend to order/ordering?

Joining sentences + relative clauses

1 **Identifying relative clauses** identify which person or thing is meant. Notice the **lack of commas**:

Mr Brown is the man who spoke to you yesterday.

Employees are loyal to a company that values its staff.

What is the greatest problem which faces business people today?

A company whose employees are unhappy is not going to keep its best staff for long.

This is the stage of the process where I always press the wrong button.

When *who, that* or *which* is the **object** of the relative clause it can be omitted:

Typing is a skill (that) everyone in business should learn.

The person (who) you spoke to is no longer with us.

This is a product (which) I'm sure your customers will want to buy.

Notice that *whom* can be used in formal writing but is uncommon in informal writing and conversation.

Instead of: we'd normally say:

The person to whom you spoke was . . .   The person you spoke to was . . .

The people with whom I am working . . .   The people I'm working with . . .

The man from whom I received the letter . . .   The man I got the letter from . . .

2 **Non-identifying relative clauses** give extra information. They are often used to join sentences and are more common in writing than in speech. Notice that *that* is not used in these clauses – and notice the use of commas:

Mr Green, who is the chief accountant, is an extraordinary man.

Our new ZX 400, which went on sale last month, is going to be a big success.

Mr White, who took over from Mr Black, has worked here for ten years.

Kerry Smith, whose boss is now Mr White, used to work for Mr Black.

3 Sentences can be joined by using these conjunctions:

Time conjunctions: *and · before · after · while · as*

Reason, cause or consequence conjunctions: *and · because · as · so that · so . . . that · such a . . . that*

Contrast conjunctions: *but · although · even though*

I took some work with me so that I would have something to do on the journey.

I read the reports while I was on the train.

The report was so badly written that I couldn't understand it.

It was such a long report that I didn't bother to finish reading it.

Even though I tried very hard, I didn't manage to finish the work.

4 Sentences can also be joined by using these prepositions:

Time prepositions: *before · after · during*

Reason, cause or consequence prepositions: *because of · due to*

Contrast prepositions: *in spite of · despite*

It was impossible to concentrate because of the noise of the traffic outside.

I read the report during my journey.

In spite of spending all night reading, I wasn't able to finish the work.

To show **purpose**, a clause with *to __* can be used:

I used a dictionary to/in order to/so as to look up any unfamiliar words.

5 Two sentences can also be connected by using these conjunctions, without actually making a single sentence from the two:

Time: *Then · Afterwards · Beforehand · Meanwhile*
Reason, cause or consequence: *Consequently · Therefore · That's why · That was why*
Contrast: *However · Nevertheless*

I tried to finish the report. However, I didn't manage to.
We all read the report. Afterwards, we discussed it.
It's an interesting report. That's why I want you to read it.

Modal verbs

1 Modal verbs are used to express ideas like ability, possibility and certainty:
can · could · have to · may · might · must · need · ought to · should · will

The same ideas can also be expressed in other words:
be able to · be obliged to · it's possible that · it's unnecessary to · it's likely that

2 Modal verbs can refer to **ability**:

PRESENT OR FUTURE	PAST
Ability: can/is able to	was able to/managed to
Inability: can't/be unable to/not be able to	couldn't wasn't able to
Questions about ability: Can he?	Was he able to?

Tony can speak Spanish very well, but he can't speak Japanese.
Anne was able to do the research, but she couldn't write the report.
I was unable to finish all my work yesterday, but I hope to be able to do it tomorrow.
I couldn't finish all my work yesterday, but I hope I can tomorrow.

3 Modal verbs can refer to **possibility** and **certainty**:

PRESENT OR FUTURE	PAST
Possibility: may/might/could	may have/could have/might have
Certainty or near certainty: must	must have
Impossibility: can't/couldn't	can't have/couldn't have
Questions about possibility: Could/Might it . . . ?	Could/Might it have . . . ?

It could/may/might rain later.
I may not be able to find the documents – they may have been shredded.
If his name's Spiros, he can't be Italian – he must be Greek.
It might be difficult to get a seat at such short notice.
Jane is usually so punctual – she must have missed her train.
Her train might have been delayed. Or it might have been cancelled.

4 Modal verbs can be used when giving or refusing **permission**:

PRESENT OR FUTURE	PAST
Giving permission:	
can/may	was allowed to
Refusing permission:	
can't/mustn't	couldn't/wasn't allowed to
Questions about permission:	
Can/Could/May we . . . ?	Was he allowed to . . . ?

You can/may make notes during the presentation if you like.
Can/Could/May I finish off this work tomorrow?
We weren't allowed to board the plane until it had been refuelled.
You can't/mustn't smoke when you're in a non-smoking seat.
We couldn't ship the order because our computer system was down.

5 Modal verbs can refer to **obligation** and **responsibility**:

PRESENT OR FUTURE	PAST
Obligation or responsibility:	
must/have to/have got to/should/ought to	had to/should have
Lack of obligation or responsibility:	
don't have to/needn't	needn't have
Obligation or responsibility NOT to do something:	
can't/musn't/shouldn't/oughtn't to	wasn't allowed to/shouldn't have
Questions about obligation or responsibility:	
Must we/Have we got to/Do we have to /	Did he have to . . . ?
Should we/Ought we to/Do we need to . . . ?	

Do I have to send them a letter, or should I phone them?
You don't have to/needn't book in advance if you're going by rail.
You must/should arrive at 8:30 if you want to get a seat on the train.
You don't have to/needn't stand up on a bus unless all the seats are occupied.
Are we allowed to make personal phone calls from the office?

The passive

1 The passive is used when the person responsible for an action is **not known** or **not important**:
Beer is made from water, hops and malted barley.
I was given a watch for my birthday.
These problems will have to be solved before we can go ahead.
The results are being published on Monday.

or when we want to **avoid** mentioning the person responsible for an action:
You were asked to arrive at 8 am. (less 'personal' than: I asked you to arrive . . .)
These packages must be shipped by next Monday.

2 *By* is often used with the passive to emphasize **who** was responsible for an action:
Penicillin was discovered by Alexander Fleming.
The first CDs were marketed in 1982 by Philips and Sony.
The research is being done by a team of European scientists.

3 Often there's no great difference in meaning between a passive and an active sentence. The passive can be used to give variety to the **style** of a report, as in these examples:

> Only 17 muscles are used when you smile, but 43 are used when you frown.
> > You only use 17 muscles when you smile, but you use 43 when you frown. (more personal)
> The light bulb was invented in 1878 (by Joseph Swan).
> > Joseph Swan invented the light bulb in 1878.
> The committee will announce the names of the Nobel Prize winners in May.
> > The names of the Nobel Prize winners will be announced (by the committee) in May.

Using the passive tends to make a sentence sound **more formal** and **less personal** than an active sentence, as in these examples:

> The battery pack and charger are included in the price.
> > We include the battery pack and charger in the price.
> Your money will be refunded in full if you are not totally satisfied.
> > We will refund your money in full if you are not totally satisfied.

Past tenses

1 The **past simple** is the tense most commonly used to refer to events that happened at a particular time in the past:

> The company was founded in 1975.
> He applied for another job last month, but he didn't get it.
> We left them a message last week, but it didn't get through.

2 The **past continuous** is used to refer to activities that were interrupted or hadn't finished at the time mentioned:

> At 7:45 last night it was still raining
> It was raining when we arrived but now it has stopped.

or to refer to simultaneous events or activities:

> We were lying in the sun while she was working hard at the office.

3 *Used to* emphasizes that the activity happened frequently in the past – but that it probably no longer takes place:

> He used to smoke 20 cigarettes a day. (but he doesn't any more)
> Before the days of PCs every secretary used to use a typewriter.

4 The **present perfect simple** is used to refer to the past in these cases:
When no definite time in the past is given or known:

> I have been to Italy several times.
> He has had four jobs in two years.

When the activity began in the the past and has not yet finished:

> I have (already) read 100 pages of the book.

When the activity finished recently:

> I have (just) been to the dentist's.

The **present perfect simple** is often used with these adverbs: *just · already · never · yet · so far*

> Have you finished your work yet?
> I have never been to South America.

Remember that the **present perfect** is **not** used to refer to a **definite time** in the past and is **not** normally used in questions that begin: *When . . . ?*
We always use the **past simple** with phrases like these:
last month · in July · on Wednesday · yesterday · a few minutes ago

I sent them a letter last week. ✓	NOT: I have sent them a letter last week. ✗
We received the shipment on Monday. ✓	NOT: We have received the shipment on Monday. ✗
When did you go there? ✓	NOT: When have you gone there? ✗

5 The **present perfect continuous** is used to emphasize that an activity started in the past and is still going on. It's commonly used with *for* or *since*:
> He has been working for the same company since he was 18.
> She has been feeling unwell for two days.

6 The **past perfect** is normally used to emphasize that one past event happened before another:
> Before he joined our company, he had never worked so hard.
> I hadn't realized he was married until I noticed his wedding ring.
> I had been feeling quite depressed until my boss told me she was impressed with my work.

and is very common in **reported speech**:

'I went there last year.'	→	He said that he had been there the previous year.
'I've been there once.'	→	She said that she had been there once.
'I paid you the money yesterday.'	→	He told her that he'd paid her the money the day before.
'I was waiting for your call.'	→	She said that she had been waiting for my call.

Phrasal verbs and Verbs + prepositions

Notice the correct (✓) and incorrect (✗) word order in each of the examples below.

1 A **verb + preposition** is followed by a noun or pronoun. You can sometimes guess the meaning of a verb + preposition from its parts:

look for (= try to find)
> I'm looking for my keys, but I can't find them. ✓

BUT NOT:
> I'm looking my keys for, but I can't find them. ✗

look at (= observe)
> I looked at the instructions for a long time, but I couldn't understand them. ✓

BUT NOT:
> I looked the instructions at for a long time . . . ✗

Some verbs + preposition have an **idiomatic** meaning and it's hard to guess their meanings from their parts:

look after (= care for)
> I looked after the arrangements. ✓ I looked after them. ✓ They were looked after by me. ✓

BUT NOT:
> I looked the arrangements after. ✗ I looked them after. ✗

Other examples: *see to · see through · do without · make for · get over*

2 A **transitive phrasal verb** (verb + adverb) is followed by a noun or pronoun. Notice how the word order is different from the examples above:

look up (= find information)
   I looked up a word. ✓   I looked a word up. ✓   I looked it up. ✓   The word was looked up. ✓
   BUT NOT:
   I looked up it. ✗

Other examples: *see off · do up · make up · find out · give away · give back*

3 An **intransitive phrasal verb** (verb + adverb) is **not** followed by a noun or pronoun:

look out (= be careful)
   You must look out! ✓
   BUT NOT:
   You were looked out. ✗

Other examples: *run away · fall over · get out · get up · give up*

4 A **phrasal verb + preposition** (verb + adverb + preposition) is followed by a noun or pronoun:

look up to (= respect)
   I look up to my boss. ✓   I look up to her. ✓   She was looked up to by everyone. ✓
   BUT NOT:
   I look my boss up to. ✗   I look her up to. ✗

Other examples: *look forward to · look out for · make off with · make up for · run away with · run out of*

Present tenses

There are four present tenses:
present simple	She lives in London.
present continuous	She's living in London.
present perfect simple	She has lived in London all her life.
present perfect continuous	She has been living in London for a few years.

1 The **present simple** describes general truths, complete events and unchanging or regular events or actions:
   Water freezes at 0° Celsius.
   I always have sugar in my coffee.
   Where do you live? (= What is your permanent address?)
   After lunch I sometimes have a cup of black coffee.

Some common **adverbs** that are often used with the **present simple** are:
   always · usually · often · generally · normally · frequently · never · hardly ever · sometimes · occasionally

2 The **present continuous** describes events happening at this moment or which haven't finished happening:
   I'm trying to concentrate, so please don't interrupt.
   Where are you living? (= What is your temporary address?)
   This year I'm doing an English language course.

Some common **adverbs** that are often used with the **present continuous** are:
   at the moment · today · this morning · this week · this month · this year · now

3   Some verbs (**stative verbs**) are not normally used in the continuous form, because they usually refer to permanent states or situations:

How much does this cost? ✔	How much is this costing? ✗
He has owned a car for two years. ✔	He has been owning a car for two years. ✗

Here are some common **stative verbs**:

believe · contain · cost · deserve · fit · know · like · look like · love · matter · owe
realize · remember · seem · smell · suit · understand

How much do I owe you?
He deserves to do well in the interview.
Do you believe me?

4   The **present perfect simple** refers to actions or situations that began in the past and which are still true or relevant now, or are now finished:

I've never smoked a cigar in my life.
Someone has used all the paper.
I haven't seen them for a long time.
Have you finished your meal?

The **present perfect continuous** refers to actions or events which started in the past and haven't finished happening, or repeated actions:

We've been waiting for twenty minutes.
What have you been doing since we last met?
I have been learning English for five years.
The phone has been ringing for a long time but nobody has answered it.

The **present perfect** is often used with these **adverbs**:

ever · so far · never · this year · this week · all my life · recently · for a long time · since 1995

For is used with a period of time:

for two years · for a long time · for a few minutes · for the last three days

Since is used with a point in time:

since 1988 · since yesterday · since 5 o'clock · since lunchtime · since April

We can't say: since two years ✗ since three days ✗

5   Although present tenses often refer to **present time**, they can also refer to **future time**:

When does this meeting end?
I'll phone you when I arrive.
When are you meeting the committee?

and **past time**:

I've been to the USA several times.
Interest rates rise in USA. (newspaper headline)

Questions and question tags

1 *Yes/No* **questions** expect the answer *Yes, No* or *I don't know. Yes/No* questions usually end with a rising tone ($\nearrow$). Notice the word order and the use of *do* and *did* in these examples:

$\nearrow$
Do you like sports?
Are you feeling all right?
Have you ever been to Spain?
Did you see the news on TV last night?

A **negative** *Yes/No* **question** may be a surprised reaction to what someone has said or done, or a question which expects the answer *Yes*:

Aren't you Tom's assistant?
– That's right, yes.
I thought so. Didn't I speak to you on the phone the other day?
– Oh yes, I remember.

2 *Wb–* **questions** ask for specific information, and can't be answered with *Yes* or *No. Wb–* **questions** usually end with a falling tone ($\searrow$). Notice the word order and use of *do* and *did* in these examples:

$\searrow$
Who did you write to?
What does she do for a living?
Where have you put my keys?
When did you see them last?

Who . . ., What . . . or *Which . . .* can also be the subject of the sentence. Notice the word order (*do* or *did* are not used in these cases):

Who wrote to you?
What surprised you most about their reaction?
Which of the letters seems more urgent?

3 It is sometimes more polite to use an **indirect question** rather than a direct question. Notice the word order in these examples:

How old are you?	May I ask how old you are?
Where do you live?	Could you tell me where you live?
Are you feeling all right?	I'd like to know if/whether you're feeling all right.
Where is the toilet?	Do you know where the toilet is?

4 **Question tags** are used to check if we are correct, by asking another person to confirm if we are right or not. There are two **intonations**:

$\nearrow$ $\searrow$
Your name's Leo, isn't it?   falling intonation = I'm fairly sure.
(The listener will probably agree.)

$\searrow$ $\nearrow$
Your surname's Jones, isn't it?   rising intonation = I'm not sure.
(The listener will confirm whether or not you're right.)

A positive verb is followed by a negative question tag, and a negative verb is followed by a positive question tag, as in these examples:

The shops will be closed by now, won't they?	They won't open again till 9 o'clock, will they?
They always close at 6 pm, don't they?	Most shops don't open on Sundays, do they?
She must be more careful, mustn't she?	He mustn't be so careless, must he?
We have to reply immediately, don't we?	You haven't finished yet, have you?

Reported speech

1 In reported speech the tense usually changes back into the past or past perfect:

'I haven't watched the news on TV for ages.' → He said that he hadn't watched the news on TV for ages.

'I don't often read the newspaper.' → She said that she didn't often read the newspaper.

'I'll phone you when I get to the office.' → He said that he would phone me when he got to the office.

'Why are you looking so surprised?' → She asked me why I was looking so surprised.

But if the information is still relevant or true, the tense needn't be changed:

My boss refused to let me know whether I'm going to get a pay rise next year.
We were told that Microsoft is the world's largest software company.

2 Reported **statements** are introduced by verbs like these, and can be followed by *that*:

add · admit · announce · answer · complain · explain · find out · inform someone · let someone know
reply · report · say · shout · suggest · tell someone · whisper

'I'm afraid I made a mistake.' → She admitted that she had made a mistake.

'Oh, and I'm sorry.' → She added that she was sorry.

'Listen everyone: we're getting married!' → They announced that they were getting married.

Reported **orders, promises, offers, requests** and **advice** are introduced by verbs like these, followed by *to ___* :

advise · ask · encourage · invite · offer · order · persuade · promise · recommend
remind · tell · threaten · want · warn

'You'd better be careful.' → She advised me to be careful.

'Will you help me, please?' → He asked me to help him.

'Don't drop it.' → She warned me not to drop it.

'Go on, have another try.' → She encouraged me to try again.

Reported **questions** are introduced by verbs like these, followed by a *Wb–* question word.
Yes/No questions are reported with *if* or *whether*:

ask · inquire · try to find out · wonder · want to know

'What are you doing?' → He asked me what I was doing.

'Are you feeling all right?' → She asked me if/whether I was feeling all right.

3 When you're reporting **times** and **places**, words like these may have to be changed:

here → there	now → then	this → that
tomorrow → the next day	yesterday → the day before	this week → that week
last week → the week before	next week → the week after	

(reporting the next day)

Some days ago she said, 'Phone them tomorrow.' → She told me to phone them the next day.

Yesterday she said, 'Send them a fax tomorrow.' → She told me to send them a fax today.

Don't forget to include this information. → She reminded me to include that information.

4 The exact words used in the original conversation are usually **summarized** in reported speech:

'I wonder if you'd mind helping me?' → She asked me to help her.

'Why don't we have lunch together?' → He invited me to have lunch.

Transcripts

Unit 1 A2

Mr Black: Er…are you Ms Robinson?
Ms Robinson: Yes, I am.
Mr Black: Oh, good morning. It's good to meet you at last.
Ms Robinson: Well, hello, Mr Black. How are you?
Mr Black: Oh, I'm fine, thank you. And you?
Ms Robinson: Well, I'm very well.
Mr Black: So, did you have a good journey?
Ms Robinson: Well, apart from an hour's delay at JFK, not too bad.
Mr Black: Oh, good, good. So tell me, did you have any difficulty finding the office?
Ms Robinson: No, no, the directions you gave me were very clear. I got a taxi from the hotel, though.
Mr Black: Oh, good. Well, tell me, is this your first visit to Paris?
Ms Robinson: Yes, it is. I'm so looking forward to doing some sightseeing later on.
Mr Black: Well, yes, it is a very beautiful city. Er…would you like some coffee?
Ms Robinson: Oh, yes, please!

Mr Green: Ms Bristow? Hi, I'm Dick Green.
Ms Bristow: Mr Green, hello, it's good to see you. How's it going?
Mr Green: Oh, fine, thanks. How are you?
Ms Bristow: I'm fine, thanks. It's good to meet you. How was your journey?
Mr Green: Oh, OK. No problems at all.
Ms Bristow: And did you manage to find us all right?
Mr Green: Oh, yes, sure, I got a taxi from the airport – it only took half an hour.
Ms Bristow: Oh good. So…um…have you had lunch?
Mr Green: Er…no, we only got breakfast on the plane, so I'm pretty hungry right now.
Ms Bristow: OK. Well, there's a very good place around the corner. Do you like Mexican food?
Mr Green: Oh, yes, I sure do . . .

Unit 1 B3

Kim: Oh, good afternoon, are you Mr Jones?
Mr Jones: Yes, good afternoon. I'm here to see Kim Wilson.
Kim: Hello, Mr Jones. I'm Kim Wilson. I'm pleased to meet you.
Mr Jones: It's nice to meet you too, Kim.
Kim: Welcome to London. Oh, would you like to sit down?
Mr Jones: Oh, yeah, thanks.
Kim: Can I get you something to drink? Um…some coffee or tea?
Mr Jones: Oh, yes, please, could I have some coffee?
Kim: Would you like it with milk?
Mr Jones: Oh, no, thanks, black, please, without sugar.
Kim: All right. And…er…would you like something to eat?
Mr Jones: No, no thanks, I'm all right, I had lunch on the plane.
Kim: Oh, yes, how was your journey?
Mr Jones: Oh, you know, not too bad. It was a bit of a bumpy flight, but we arrived on time.
Kim: Good. And you managed to find us all right?
Mr Jones: Yeah, yeah, thanks to the little map you sent me, I got here quite easily.
Kim: Good. Here's your coffee, Mr Jones.
Mr Jones: Thanks. . . . Ooh, that's very nice. Do call me Bill, by the way.
Kim: OK, fine. Is this your first visit to . . .

Unit 2 A2

Charles Cotton: My name's…er…Charles Cotton. Um…I'm the chief executive officer of Virata Corporation and our company…er…designs and markets…er…semi-conductors and software, which are used by equipment manufacturers to make the Internet experience much faster.
    Our Head Office is in Santa Clara, so I spend probably about 60% of my time in…er…in California, in Silicon Valley. We're 400 people, we are a global company with operations in all of the major continents in the world. Um…and we're part of one of the fastest growing markets that's…er…ever existed. Um…so it…it's very satisfying to see how we've been able to be successful in that environment and to see…um…the way in which we're helping to change the nature of communications in the future, and I think that's both very exciting and also very satisfying.

Peter Callaghan: My name is Peter Callaghan. Er…I'm an Australian by birth. I call myself a 'company doctor', which is taking on businesses that are in need of rapid change, it's normally about turning around companies that are not performing (well) from a profit point of view.
    The most interesting part, the bit…the part that I really like to see is, is seeing the people change. What I have learnt is how to get people to be realistic about what their strengths and weaknesses are, to get them committed to making change quickly and…er…it's very rewarding when…when people actually take that on and make a change in the business. And I could normally do that…um…in a fairly short period of time. I've got some techniques I've developed over the years, that I get people engaged in the…in the process of change very quickly. And if they can't change, I have a saying: 'If you can't change the people, you have to change the people!' Haha! So those who won't change…um…change another way. They have to go.

Unit 2 A3

Charles: I would typically get up at five o'clock, I'd go out for a run, er…h…have some breakfast, be in the office by seven and then probably a…a lot of meetings. Um…I spend a lot of time when I'm in (the) California, working with people inside the company on things like the…the way the business is going, the strategic development. And then people outside the company, particularly investors, perhaps companies that we're interested to form new relationships with.
    Probably on average (I) have eighty to a hundred e-mails every day, and that takes, even though, you know, some don't need answers . . . E-mail is like a conversation, although it's asynchronous, you don't talk to somebody exactly in real time. They send you an e-mail because they want a response fairly quickly. That takes an amount of attention and there are obviously lots of phone calls and so on as well.

Peter: I would probably start…er…about nine o'clock. I don't switch on a computer first thing. Um…I'm normally…I'm talking to someone either by telephone or face to face. That's how I would start the day. I don't have a lot of mail. Um…but I would normally start fairly early in the day with a re…with review meetings on different projects – I have project teams working on different things. And I probably have through the course of a day two or three meetings…er…on specific projects and…um…at the end of those meetings I would write the minutes of the meetings and then move on to the next mee…meeting.

Unit 3 A2

Charles: I…I think that…um…people are very disciplined about their…their working days, they're disciplined about their time. They, during the working week, um…typically work at least a twelve-hour day and…er…potentially longer than that. Um…you know, senior people in the company are probably starting e-mails at…er…before seven o'clock in the morning, or making phone calls before seven o'clock, particularly where they're making phone calls either to Asia or to…to Europe because of the time difference. Um…so…and typically, you know, perhaps finishing at seven or eight o'clock in the evening or even later if there's evening meetings to be had. And then you find that most Californians are tucked up in bed by, at (the) latest, by ten o'clock so that they can then be up early in the morning.

Californians started this sort of 'dress down Friday' …er…programme and that sort of has gone now to a situation where it's 'dress down' most days! And I think we're starting to see things coming out the other side now, where actually people are starting to dress up. So in fact people are starting to go to meetings and wearing a collar and tie again!

Narrator: You're Chief Executive Officer. Do people call you Mr Cotton?

Charles: Haha! No, it's very, very informal and I think that informality now…um…travels across the globe in technology companies. And I…I think technology companies tend to have introduced a more relaxed working environment, we have a very flat organization so…um…there is not a lot of hierarchy. It's very important in young, well in *all* companies, to…er…have excellent communications.

Some of the things that we do for instance is that, you know, we have a get-together on a Friday afternoon and, you know, there will beer and crisps and nuts and so on brought in and…er…it's a…it's a common sort of thing . A so-called 'beer bash', which started off in California has spread into other locations. And it's all about it…a means for…um…or an environment within which you can have some informal…um…communications. It's…it's used as an opportunity to update everybody in the company about what's going on in areas that they may not be associated with. And that's very important, particularly in a…in a company like ours which has got many, many locations.

Isabel Boira Segarra: In Spain they've got lots of public holidays, we don't. Um…although they have to take most of the…in a lot of places they…they have to take most of the summer vacation in the summer, in August, as a block. Here we don't have any requirement to take holidays any time of the year. I think we have two days at Christmas that we have to take because the office shuts for a week. Apart from that we can do what we like with our holidays. In Spain a lot of people have to take August off. Um…but then they get a lot of public holidays, really a lot of public holidays, which is lovely. They…there's something they call a 'bridge'. If a public holiday falls on a Tuesday they might take Monday off, if it falls on a Thursday they might take Friday off. And if…there is a week in November I think it is that there is a holiday either side of the week, so most people just disappear for the week!

I think we…well, Spanish people are much more relaxed about time, and maybe things are changing, but my impression is that things take place at a lower pace to some extent than they do here. That would be a difference. Um…a…an important difference now to do with the atmosphere at work is the…um…in Spain there's a lot of smoke in offices, where…there…here they are non-smoking offices. I find that a striking difference. I think it's bound to be because Spanish people are different to English people. We are more…we are louder, more physical. So I reckon it's probably much more noisy in Spain than it is in England. I have to keep remembering to keep my voice down!

Unit 4 B2

Jerry: Hi, Jane.

Jane: Hi Jerry. Oh, it's…is there something wrong?

Jerry: Yes, I'm trying to make some copies but I think there's a paper jam in the photocopier.

Jane: Oh…er…would you…er…like me to see what I can do?

Jerry: Oh, yes, OK.

Jane: All right. I think this is what needs doing. I'll just lift the lid . . . Oh, yeah, the paper's jammed, this sheet is crumpled. Look, I'll just get it get it out . . . There we are. Then if we close the lid, it should be OK.

Jerry: Oh, great. Thank you very much. I've got masses of copies to make.

Jane: Oh, do you…do you mind if I make a couple of copies first? It won't take long.

Jerry: No, of course not.

Jane: Thanks . . . One, two. There we are. All done. It's all yours.

Jerry: I hope it doesn't go wrong again!

Jane: Yeah, so do I. Good luck. See you later.

Jerry: Thanks for fixing it. Bye now.

Unit 5 A2

Tom White: . . . I'm sorry, could you say that again?

Ms Brown: Is it available in different colours?

Tom: Different colours?

Ms Brown: Yes.

Tom: Well, er…no…er…there's just this one colour. Pale grey. Er…well, I think you'll find it blends with your other equipment.

Ms Brown: I'm not so sure. Can you tell me about compatibility?

Tom: I…I'm sorry, I didn't quite catch what you said.

Ms Brown: Compatible. Is it compatible with Macintosh as well as Windows?

Tom: Oh, um…yeah…yes, it's…it's fully compatible.

Ms Brown: And what about speed?

Tom: S…sorry, I…I…I'm not quite sure what you mean.

Ms Brown: Speed. How long does it take to scan a document and convert it into text?

Tom: Ah! Oh, I see, yes. Er…w…say an average one-page document would take two and half minutes.

Ms Brown: Hmm, and I need to know about the footprint.

Tom: Do you mean h…how much space it occupies on a desk?

Ms Brown: Yes.

Tom: Er…it's…er…25 centimetres wide and 35 centimetres deep, but you need to allow an extra, say about 10 centimetres at the back, you know, for the…for the cables.

Ms Brown: Hm. Do you know what the power consumption is?

Tom: Yes…er…

Mr Andrews: …er…no, I'm sure they'll be ready.

Lisa Wood: All right, all right, but could we just look at the various items on the order form?

Mr Andrews: Yeah, sure. They'll all be…er…you know, er…ready in a few days…er…

Lisa: So, do you mean the whole shipment will be ready at the end of this week?

Mr Andrews: Well, yeah. No, maybe not quite then, because…um…

Lisa: All right, s…so you can tell me which items will be ready and which won't be ready?

Mr Andrews: Yeah, well, er…the…er…B450's we have in stock, so…er…no problem there. And the C24's are coming in tomorrow. So it's just the D49's really.

Lisa: So the B450's are ready now?

Mr Andrews: Well, it…they…how many did you order?

Lisa: 70 boxes.

Mr Andrews: Did you say 70 or 17 boxes?

Lisa: Seven O.

Mr Andrews: Oh, I see, well, I'm not sure how many we do have in stock. The people in the warehouse would have that information…

Lisa: Oh, well…

Unit 5 A3

Ms Brown: …Do you know what the power consumption is?

Tom: Yes…er… Look, here's a brochure all about it. You know, just…just read through it and then I'll be happy to answer any questions you've got.

Mr Andrews: …Oh, I see, well I'm not sure how many we do have in stock. The people in the warehouse would have that information.

Lisa: Oh, well… Look, if you don't know, why don't you just say so?

Unit 5 B2

1

Ms A: OK, what I'm not sure about is the price. What I want to find out is the price we pay from the distributor and also the price to the end-user in the shops.

2

Mr B: I have to go now otherwise I'll miss my train. But if you want to get in touch, give me a call at the office tomorrow. The extension number is 5844. Must go!

3

Ms C: If there are any problems, please get in touch with my assistant, Henri Duvalier. That's Henri, HENRI, Duvalier, DUVALIER.

4

Mr D: So, we'll need 45 boxes of the 30 amp transformers right away and another 15 in a week's time. Is that OK?

5

Ms E: OK, today's the 15th, we need to get the final contract to Excelsior International by the 14th of next month. Can you make sure that's done?

6

Mr F: Could you make copies of these documents and get someone to bring them round to me at my hotel this afternoon. I'm at the Kingsway on the seafront.

7

Ms G: OK, I'll just tell you the numbers: the serial number is one-four one-two zero-two and the product code is one-two one-four two-zero. Got that?

Unit 6 A2

Jane Morris: Hello.

Man: Is that Celia Sharpe?

Jane: No, she's not here.

Man: Oh, um…any idea when she'll be back?

Jane: Mm, haven't a clue. Er…can you call back later?

Man: Well, when should I call?

Jane: Er…well, probably tomorrow might be best. Oh, she's sure to be here then.

Man: Er…all right then, I will. Goodbye.

Jane: Bye.

Jane: Hello, Cinderella International. Jane Morris, speaking, how may I help you?

Man: Oh, hello, Jane. Um…I wanted to speak to Celia Sharpe.

Jane: Ms Sharpe? I'm sorry but she's not available at the moment.

Man: Er…any idea when she will be available?

Jane: Not for the rest of the day, I'm afraid. Um…is there anything I can do for you? Um…or would you like to leave a message?

Man: Er…no, it's OK. Just tell her I'll ring her tomorrow morning would you, please. My name's Bob Johnson.

Jane: All right, Mr Johnson, that's fine. I'll leave a message on her desk.

Man: Thank you. Er…bye.

Jane: Thank you, Mr Johnson. Thank you for calling. Bye-bye.

Unit 6 B1

Peter Blake: Good morning. How may I help you?

Woman: Hello, is that the Export Department?

Peter: Yes, this is Peter Blake speaking.

Woman: Oh, hello, Mr Blake. It's actually Tina MacDonald I want to speak to.

Peter: I'm sorry, she's not here just now.

Woman: Oh, how annoying. I really need to get something sorted out.

Peter: Is there anything I can do to help?

Woman: Well, let me explain the problem…

Mandy Green: Good morning, Compass International.

Mr Eastwood: Oh, er…is that the Export Department?

Mandy: Yes, this is Mandy Green speaking.

Mr Eastwood: Oh, er…this is Tim Eastwood. Er…is Mrs MacDonald available?

Mandy: Oh! Oh, Mr Eastwood. I'm sorry, but she's not here just now.

Mr Eastwood: Oh, any idea when she'll be back?

Mandy: Mm, well, I'm afraid she's not back till Monday. Can I give her a message?

Mr Eastwood: Mm, oh, can I get her on her cell phone?

Mandy: Well, yes, you could try that. Do you know the number?

Unit 7 B1

Man: …Mr Turner's not here. Can I take a message?

Mme Pineau: Yes, please tell Mr Turner that his order number 5…456 is going to be delayed until next Friday.

Man: Order 456.

Mme Pineau: Yes. The shipment will leave us here in Paris on Friday morning and it will arrive at your warehouse on Monday afternoon.

Man: Shipment leaving Paris on Friday morning, arriving here when?

Mme Pineau: Monday afternoon. Now, if Mr Turner has any questions, he can phone me on my mobile number: 0789 983 501.

Man: He can phone you on 0789 983 510.

Mme Pineau: No, no, that's 0789 983 501.

Man: OK, I've got that. Thank you, Madame Pineau.

Mme Pineau: I'm sorry about the delay, but there is nothing I can do about it.

Woman: . . . so can I note down the details so that we get everything exactly right?

Mr Lee: Yes, certainly. I'll be leaving here on May 1st arriving in Springfield on the 2nd at 12:30 pm. That's a Tuesday.

Woman: Right, 12:30 on Tuesday May 2nd.

Mr Lee: Yes.

Woman: What's the flight number?

Mr Lee: Mm...CX 301.

Woman: Right, CX 301.

Mr Lee: Correct.

Woman: Well, I'll be there to meet you at the airport.

Mr Lee: Good. And can you book me a non-smoking room for four nights at the Hilton Hotel?

Woman: OK, four nights at the Hilton. So you're leaving on Saturday the 6th?

Mr Lee: Yes. And...er...can you please e-mail me to confirm that this room is booked?

Woman: OK. What is your e-mail address?

Mr Lee: It's 'jlee@rainbow.com.hk'.

Woman: OK, 'jlee@rainbow.com.hk'.

Mr Lee: Right.

Woman: OK, Mr Lee, I'll do that right away. Now, if the Hilton isn't available, is the Marriott OK?

Mr Lee: Oh, yes, certainly.

Woman: OK, all right. Well, thank you for calling, Mr Lee.

Mr Lee: Goodbye.

Woman: Bye.

Unit 8 A1

Joe: 579814. Can I help you?

Emily: Hello, this is Emily Harris.

Joe: Hello, Emily. Er...Joe White here.

Emily: Oh, hello, Joe. Um...is Susan there?

Joe: Ah, no, no, she's...er...she's not in today, I'm afraid. Is there anything I can do?

Emily: No...um...that's OK. Er...could I leave her a message, please?

Joe: Yeah, of course.

Emily: Now, can you tell her that the team meeting on Monday has had to be postponed? Can she find out if it's possible to change it to Tuesday morning please? The best starting time for me would be . . . 11 o'clock?

Joe: Right, OK, Tuesday at 11 am.

Emily: Yeah, and please remind her that she needs to book the Meeting Room with seating for, oh, let's say a dozen people.

Joe: OK, right, er...should we arrange lunch in the canteen?

Emily: Oh, no, no. Um...can you ask Susan to arrange for drinks. Er...coffee and cold drinks – oh, and some sandwiches. Then we can continue the meeting over lunch if we need to. Oh, and the meeting has to finish by 2 o'clock because I have an appointment in the afternoon.

Joe: OK, yeah, right, that's fine. I've got all that. Um...now, I won't be here tomorrow myself to tell her this, right, so...um...what I'm going to do is just leave a message on her desk.

Emily: Lovely, fine, thanks Joe.

Joe: You're welcome, Emily.

Unit 8 C1

Max Fischer: . . . Could I leave a message for Barbara Black, please? I'm away from my desk right now, so I can't e-mail her with all this.

Woman: Um...that's OK, I'll put the message on her desk

before I leave. She'll see it before she leaves the office.

Max: OK. Well, we've had to rearrange the schedule for her visit here to Berlin tomorrow.

Woman: OK.

Max: Er...she was going to start at 9, but the first appointment is now 8:30. So, I'll pick her up at...er...7 o'clock from the hotel.

Woman: 'First appointment now 8:30. Picking her up at 7.'

Max: Right. And...er...so, the second appointment has been brought forward to 9:15. Please remind her to bring plenty of catalogues with her.

Woman: 'Second appointment 9:15', OK. How many catalogues should she bring?

Max: Oh, about 20 should be enough. Then there are no changes to the rest of the morning. That's all according to the original schedule.

Woman: 'Rest of the morning. No change.'

Max: Then lunch. She knows that Herr Müller is going to be there, but now Frau Doktor Schmidt is also going to be there.

Woman: 'Frau Doktor Schmidt' – is that S C H M I D T?

Max: Yes. Er...then in the afternoon – Barbara will be pleased about this – I've managed to arrange for a tour of the factory and the warehouse. And then we'll book her a taxi at 4 pm to get her back to the airport an hour before her flight at 5:45.

Woman: 'Taxi at 16:00.' Is there a contact number where she can reach you if there are any problems?

Max: Er...yes, she can call me on my cell phone. Er...the number is 0187 893 1291.

Woman: Er...could you say the number again more slowly, please?

Max: Sorry, sure! Er...it's 0 1 8 7 8 9 3 1 2 9 1.

Woman: '0187 893 1291.'

Max: That's right.

Woman: OK, I've got that. I'll make sure . . .

Unit 8 C2

Barbara Black: Hello, this is Barbara Black. Max Fischer isn't answering his cell phone, so I'm leaving you this message for him. I got Max's message about the changes to the Berlin schedule. And, you see, I'm afraid I've...I've got a problem: my flight to Berlin has been cancelled. This means I...I'm not going to arrive till 10 am tomorrow. Can you ask Max to cancel the first two appointments and rearrange them for the afternoon – either before or after the factory visit? I've changed my return flight to 20:45, so there's...there's plenty of time. Please ask Max call me back first to tell me he's got this message, and then...then again to confirm that he's made the arrangements. My number is 0044 1222 76198. That's 0044 1222 76198.

Unit 9 A1

Sarah Bryant: Tip-top Products, how can I help you?

Alan: Oh, hello, er...can I speak to Sarah Bryant, please?

Sarah: Well, this is she.

Alan: Oh, right, good. Er...now, look the reason why I'm calling you is to find out a few things about your order. Um...now where is it? Er...let me just find the relevant . . . Ah, yes, here we are.

Sarah: Er...is this going to take long? I was just leaving the office.

Alan: Oh, no, no, no, it won't take long. Just a few questions.

Sarah: All right. Go ahead.

Alan: Right, now...er...first, you haven't filled out the

space where it says 'Colour'. Which colour would you like us to send you?

Sarah: Well, what colours are there?

Alan: What? Oh…er…I'll just have to have a look at the catalogue. Er…that's page 12…no, page 14 . . . erm…yep, here we are. The colours are blue and…er…and…and…and blue. Oh, it's only available in blue. Oh, I'm sorry.

Sarah: That's OK. Anything else you want to know?

Alan: Well, yes, er…there was something else, now what was it? It…er…no, I'm sorry it's gone. Oh, wait, no, I remember. I don't have your e-mail address.

Sarah: OK. Well, it's…er: 'sbryant@ . . .'

Alan: 'sybryant' . . . Oh, hang on, wait just a moment, my pen's not working, I . . . No, it's OK now. S…sorry, could you start again please?

Sarah: Yes. 'sbryant@tip-top.com' – that's S B R Y A N T at T I P dash T O P dot com.

Alan: Ah, right, yes, thank you. If I think of anything else, can I call you later?

Sarah: Well, not really, I'm just leaving. It's 6 o'clock here you know.

Alan: Is it? Oh, I didn't realize. Oh, I am sorry.

Sarah: Well, that's OK. Bye.

Alan: Bye, Ms Bryant.

Unit 9 B1

Elliot Taylor: Hello?

Rebecca King: Hello, can I speak to Mr Taylor, please?

Elliot: This is he.

Rebecca: Good. I'm just updating our records. We want to be quite sure that our database is correct and up-to-date.

Elliot: Yes?

Rebecca: So, can I ask you a few questions?

Elliot: Er…sorry, who am I speaking to, please?

Rebecca: This is Rebecca King, Mr Taylor.

Elliot: Oh, right. I didn't recognize your voice. Er…so, what's the problem?

Rebecca: I just need some information to update our database. It won't take very long. First, can you tell me your e-mail address?

Elliot: Yes, certainly. It's 'etaylor@velocity-audio-studios.com'.

Rebecca: OK, and do you have a website?

Elliot: Yes, it's 'www.velocity-audio-studios.com'.

Rebecca: Right. And do you have a fax number?

Elliot: Yes, it's 001 815 983 4518.

Rebecca: Thanks. OK that's everything. Goodbye Mr Taylor.

Elliot: Goodbye . . . *[phone goes dead]* . . . Miss King.

Olivia Sutton: Hello, how can I help you?

Nick Burgess: Hello, can I speak to Olivia Sutton, please?

Olivia: Speaking.

Nick: Oh, hello. My name is Nick Burgess. I'm calling about your order number B 434.

Olivia: B 434? Is there a problem?

Nick: No, not at all. Just a query really.

Olivia: Oh, OK, what do you want to know?

Nick: It's just that we've recently updated the specification for the Classic range and we now have a new model coming out. I wonder if you'd prefer to order that instead of the older model.

Olivia: Oh. Um…is there a price difference?

Nick: Well, yes, but the new price is only 5% higher, but the performance is much better.

Olivia: Oh, I see. Well, look, could you fax the new specifications to me, and then I can take a close look and decide?

Nick: Certainly. Would you like me to put your order

B 434 on hold until you've decided?

Olivia: Oh, can you do that?

Nick: Yes, of course, that's no problem at all.

Olivia: All right.

Nick: I think you'll be impressed by the new specifications. I'll fax them through to you now.

Olivia: Oh, good. Thanks very much.

Nick: Thanks. Bye.

Unit 10 A1

Jack Connolly: Hello, Jack Connolly, speaking

Sandra Perry: Oh, hello, this is Sandra Perry. You promised to e-mail me with that information yesterday.

Jack: Oh, yes, I know. I tried to, but my e-mails kept coming back marked 'undeliverable'.

Sandra: Well, what was the address you used?

Jack: 'sperry@xanadu.com'.

Sandra: No, no, no, that's the old address. I gave you the new one on my last e-mail to you.

* * *

Jack: Oh, I'm terribly sorry about that.

Sandra: That's all right, it's all right. Can you try again?

Jack: Yes, of course. Er…could you please tell me your new e-mail address?

Sandra: It's sperry@xanadu.co.uk .

Jack: OK. I'll update m…my address book right away and send you the e-mail in a couple of minutes . . .

Unit 10 A2

David Shaw: David Shaw.

Jenny: Hello, Mr Shaw, I…um…promised to call you yesterday.

David: Yes, I was waiting for your call, what happened?

Jenny: Well, I had a lot of trouble compiling the figures. You see, my computer crashed and it took the rest of the day to fix it.

David: So, why didn't you call me this morning?

* * *

Jenny: I tried calling you this morning but the line was busy all the time.

David: Oh, I see. Well, do you have the figures now?

Jenny: Yep, here they are . . . Oh! Oh, no! Oh d . . . Do you mind if I call you back in a few minutes? My computer's just crashed again!

Unit 12 A2

Sam Morton: Hello, er…Fritz. This is Sam Morton. I…It's about our meeting on Friday. My flight gets in at 8:45 now, not 10:30. So…er…please don't bother to come and pick me up. I can easily get a taxi to the office – er…I should be there by 10 o'clock. This means we'll have an hour to talk about the project before we meet Mrs Neumann. Then we can go over to her office together at 11:30. Um…can you book a table at the Golden Gate Restaurant for the three of us for 1 o'clock? And…er…don't forget to tell them that Mrs Neumann is a vegetarian. So…er…I'll see you on Friday. I…if there are any delays I'll call you at the office. If you want to call me, my cell phone number is 0789 923 81945. OK, see you on Friday!

Unit 14 B1

Woman: Prochem Engineering, how can I help you?

Mr Chang: Hello, this is Mr Chang.

Woman: Hello, Mr Chang, thanks for calling back. Well, how can I help you?

Mr Chang: It's about the J44 prototype. I'm very worried about the faults. What are you going to do about them?

Woman: Well, we're redesigning the faulty components now. We know what's gone wrong and the redesign is nearly finished. The new prototype will be ready in a few days.

Mr Chang: I don't want it to go into production before my engineer has checked the components.

Woman: I don't think that's necessary.

Mr Chang: Oh, yes, I insist.

Woman: Fine. All right. Well, how should we proceed then?

Mr Chang: I want to send my engineer over to you to inspect everything and carry out measurements and tests. But you will have to pay his expenses for this.

Woman: Um…Yes, OK, that sounds fair. But the prototype may be ready by Friday. If it is, then our Mr Simpson can bring it with him and your team can inspect it in your factory on Monday. Well, that would save your engineer having to come all this way.

Mr Chang: That's a better idea.

Woman: The problem is that it may not be ready in time for this.

Mr Chang: Look, I'm going to be with you on Thursday myself.

Woman: Oh, well, then you could inspect it yourself!

Mr Chang: No, I'm not qualified to carry out a technical inspection. And anyway, you said it might not be ready.

Woman: That's true. OK, well, let's talk about this further on Thursday.

Mr Chang: Fine. I'm arriving at 2 o'clock . . .

Unit 19 A1

Ingrid: . . . and here's your tea, Mr Grey.

Mr Grey: Oh, thanks.

Ingrid: So, did you have a good journey?

Mr Grey: Yes.

Ingrid: Good. Mm…where do you come from?

Mr Grey: England.

Ingrid: Oh. And…er…is this your first visit to our country?

Mr Grey: No.

Ingrid: How did you travel?

Mr Grey: By plane.

Ingrid: Oh, did…did you have a good flight?

Mr Grey: Not really.

Ingrid: Is your hotel all right?

Mr Grey: Yeah, it's OK.

Ingrid: Oh. What sort of room have you got?

Mr Grey: Well, I…it's quite a large room. Th…there's a nice view of the park and, you know, there's plenty of . . .

Ingrid: Oh, good. Here's Mrs Crimson now. Mrs Crimson, this is Mr Grey!

Mrs Crimson: Hello, Mr Grey. Ingrid's been looking after you all right then . . .

Unit 19 A3

1

Karen: . . . that's fine because I think this new product will be really popular.

David: Er…so how much market research have you done?

Karen: Oh, we've spent a long time on it.

2

Karen: . . . and we found out that over 50% of our customers wanted a wider range of colours.

David: How many different colours do they want?

Karen: Six different colours, they said.

3

Karen: . . . if we drop our prices, sales will rise.

David: OK, and what did your research suggest?

Karen: We discovered that if the price goes down by 20%, our sales will rise by 50%.

4

Karen: . . . is we're going to introduce some changes.

David: Right, er…when are you going to introduce them?

Karen: Probably next year.

5

Karen: . . . we have really high hopes for this new product.

David: And do you have a name for it?

Karen: Yes, we do. It's the ZX 410.

Unit 20 A1

Terry Hughes: Morning, Jackie.

Jackie: Morning, Terry. Can I just go through the diary with you for next week?

Terry: Sure.

Jackie: Now, um…the report for Mr Pearson is due on Monday. And he wants it by 5:30 at the latest.

Terry: OK, 5.30. I don't have much time to work on it though.

Jackie: Mm, no, you're free from 9 to 11. That should be enough time.

Terry: Fine, um…what's happening at 11?

Jackie: You're meeting Mr Braun.

Terry: Oh, yes. And…er…I meant to tell you that I've arranged to have lunch with Ms Ford at 12:30.

Jackie: Oh!

Terry: Can you book us a table somewhere nice?

Jackie: Yes, sure, er…is the Palace Hotel OK?

Terry: Yes, perfect. After lunch I may have more time to work on the report if I haven't finished it.

Jackie: Mm, right. But you need to remember to call Arena International in the afternoon.

Terry: OK, I'll put that in the diary for 2:30. So, apart from giving the report to Mr Pearson at 5:30, that's it for the day?

Jackie: Uh, no, not quite. Betty Dixon is calling you at 6 pm from Seattle.

Terry: Right. Now, how about Tuesday?

Jackie: Tuesday is the brainstorming meeting with the Marketing staff.

Terry: Oh, yes. What time?

Jackie: 8:45. And at 11:15 Anne-Marie is arriving from Switzerland.

Terry: Does she need picking up?

Jackie: Oh, no, she said she'd get a taxi.

Terry: Fine. Now, let's arrange a tour of the factory for her, and lunch.

Jackie: OK, when?

Terry: The tour can be before lunch at 12, then lunch at 1 o'clock.

Jackie: In the canteen?

Terry: No, let's go to Lorenzo's. I'll ask Dick and Tony to come with us.

Jackie: OK, I'll book it. Now then, at 3:30 you're meeting Nancy and Mark.

Terry: Er…no, that's been cancelled. So I'm free all afternoon.

Jackie: Oh, not quite.

Terry: Not another report to write?

Jackie: No, you've got an appointment with the dentist at 4 pm.

Terry: Oh, lovely!

Unit 21 A2

Interviewer: So, Rob, you went to Brazil recently, didn't you?

Rob: Yes, I did, that's right.

Interviewer: So, what happened?

Rob: Well, I went into this meeting and…er…there were about, ooh, seven or eight people in there, er…and I just said 'Hello' to everybody and sat down.

Apparently, what I should have done is to go round the room shaking hands with everyone individually. Well, you know, it's silly of me because…er…I found out later it upset everyone. I mean, I…I think they felt I was taking them for granted.

Kate: Haha, well I know that because when I was in France the first time, I finished a meeting with, oh, gosh, it was about half a dozen people and I was in a hurry to leave, so I just said 'Goodbye, everyone!', you know, to all the people there. Well, I later found out that what I should have done is shake hands with everyone in the group when I left. Now, apparently, it's the polite thing to do.

Interviewer: Well, people shake hands in different ways, don't they?

Rob: Oh, yes, that's right, they do. See, normally I shake hands quite gently when I meet someone. So when I went to…w…the USA for the first time, I think people there thought my weak handshake w…was a sign of weakness. Apparently, people there tend to shake hands quite firmly.

Kate: Oh, gosh! You know, that reminds me: on my first trip to Germany, it was a long time ago, I was introduced to the boss in the company when he passed us in the corridor. Well, I wasn't prepared, and I mean, I had my left hand in my pocket. And when he…we shook hands I realized my left hand was still in my pocket. Well, that was, you know, you can imagine, very bad manners and I was quite embarrassed actually, you know.

Interviewer: And how about using first names? Er…have you made any mistakes there?

Rob: Oh, yes, I have! When I first went to Italy I thought it was OK to use everyone's first name so as to seem friendly. And then I later discovered that in business you shouldn't…erm…use someone's first name unless you are invited to. Oh, and you should always use their title (Dottore, Dottoressa or…or whatever) as well.

Kate: Hm, yeah, well, when I met people in Russia, you know, they seemed to be puzzled when I shook hands with them and said 'How do you do?' Well, what they do when they greet a stranger is to say their own name, so I had that all wrong!

Rob: Oh, yes, I agree with that. Remembering names is very important. I…I found business cards very useful when I was in Japan not so long ago. Each person can clearly see the other's name a…and the job title on the card itself. And then I, once again, found out that you have to treat business cards with respect. What you've got to do is…is hold them with both hands and then read them very carefully. What happened to me was: the first time I just took a man's card with one hand and put it straight into my pocket.

Interviewer: So, any other advice?

Kate: Well … Ha! One time, I unintentionally caused some problems when I was in Taiwan. Well, I was trying to make a joke when I pretended to criticize my business associate for being late for a meeting. And…um…I mean, he was embarrassed, I mean, he was really embarrassed instead of being amused. Now, you shouldn't criticize people in Taiwan or embarrass them. I mean, you must avoid confrontation, that's for sure!

Rob: Oh, I must tell you about the first time I was in Mexico! I…I have to admit I found it a bit strange when business associates there touched me…er…you know, just on the arm a…and the shoulder. Well, I tried to move away and, of course,

they thought I was being very, very unfriendly. Apparently, it's quite usual there for men to touch each other in, you know, in a friendly way. Oh…oh, and another thing: the first time I went to Korea I thought it was polite not to look someone in the eye too much. The Koreans I met seemed to be staring at me when I spoke, which seemed, you know, a bit odd at first. In Korea, eye contact conveys sincerity and it shows you're paying attention to the speaker.

Kate: Oh, well, it seemed strange because you British don't look at each other so much when you're talking to each other. I mean, you look away, you know, most of the time. I found this hard to deal with when I…when I first came to the UK, because people seemed to be embarrassed when I looked at them while they were speaking to me.

Interviewer: So, what's the thing visitors to Britain should avoid most?

Rob: Well, I don't think we're all that sensitive, do you, Kate?

Kate: Ohoo, well, I'll tell you, I made a big mistake when I was in Scotland. I found myself referring to the UK as 'England' and to the British as 'the English'. Now, I know … that would be just as bad in Wales, I guess, wouldn't it?

Rob: Yes, it certainly would!

Kate: Haha …

Unit 22 A1

1

Man: … I'd like to order some reclining chairs. Um…do you have…er… [someone in the office sneezes] … fifty of them in stock because that's how many we need.

2

Woman: … Look, I know that shipping can take over a week. We need them by the 19th so I want to get this order processed as soon as possible.

3

Man: … so they have to be shipped here. I suppose there will be two truck loads, but that's OK.

4

Woman: … and Deirdre Macpherson is the name of the consignee which needs to be written on the shipping note.

5

Man: … the last time we had a shipment there was some confusion about the address. The driver didn't know there's a Richmond Road and a Richmond Avenue, so he didn't find the right building.

6

Man: … Oh, yes the zip code is 89372, you'll need that on the invoice if you're mailing it.

7

Woman: … is that we have them here as soon as possible.

8

Man: … Last time we ordered 80 of them, but this year we want to increase that by another 30 if that's OK. Can you do that?

Unit 24 A2

Interviewer: Sarah!

Sarah: Yes?

Interviewer: Just before you go into your meeting, can I ask you what you think is going to happen?

Sarah: Oh, sure. Well, I'm meeting Bob – he's my counterpart from the US office. And we have to keep each other up to date on what we've been doing for the last month…er…and try to sort of co-ordinate our plans for the next month, really. Th…there'll just be the two of us, and it's my turn to take notes, unfortunately!

Interviewer: And how long is it going to last?

Sarah: Well, we've set aside an hour but, well, we usually overrun. But…that…it doesn't matter, we've got all afternoon if necessary. I don't actually foresee any problems, I mean, we usually see eye-to-eye on things, so I think it should be fairly enjoyable. But I must go. It's nearly two o'clock now.

Interviewer: OK, have a good meeting!

Sarah: Thanks.

Interviewer: Carlos!

Carlos: Oh, yeah, hi.

Interviewer: Hi. Er…before you go into your meeting, can I ask you what you think is going to happen?

Carlos: Oh, man, I'm really dreading this meeting. I mean, the other guy, the production controller, is a really tough cookie. Let's put it this way: he has strong opinions about everything, I mean, it's very hard for him to change his mind about anything. I mean, my purpose is to inform him about some changes to the system that *our* people are proposing, right. And his purpose is to stop any changes and maintain the status quo. Ha, it's going to be tough and…er…it's sure to go on for hours and hours, I mean, you know. And I…I know the assistant controller will also be there, and she always takes his side so as not to upset their working relationship. And I…I'll have to make notes so that I can report back to my team on Monday. So, er…yeah, it's going to be a great day – wish me luck!

Interviewer: Good luck!

Unit 24 A3

Interviewer: So, Sarah, how was your meeting?

Sarah: Oh, hi! It was fine. Bob's assistant was there, too, actually, but she didn't have much to say. But she did make notes, so we didn't have to, which was good. It was an easy meeting and we finished on time, surprisingly.

Interviewer: Oh, good, thank you very much.

Interviewer: So, Carlos, how was your meeting?

Carlos: Hey! Haha! OK, yeah! I think it was because he was in a good mood. He seemed very open to our ideas and he agreed to propose them to his team. Er…the assistant controller wasn't there, so that may have helped, too. So, here are my notes, er…just our list of proposals with ticks everywhere to show we agreed. And it's not even four o'clock yet. What a nice way to finish the week!

Unit 24 B1

Franz: Jan, lovely to see you!

Jan: Hello, Franz, thank you for coming.

Franz: That's OK. How are you?

Jan: I'm fine. How was your holiday?

Franz: Brilliant! We had a really great time. What about you? Are you going away this summer?

Jan: No, I haven't got time. But we went away in the spring, which was nice.

Franz: Oh, yes, I remember you telling me about it. When is your next break?

Jan: Not till Christmas.

Franz: That's a long time.

Jan: Mm. OK. Shall we start?

Franz: Sure.

Jan: Now, then, the first thing we need to talk about …

Jan: … Right, that seems fine. Is there anything else you'd like to discuss?

Franz: N…not really. I think that covers everything.

Jan: Good. And we've agreed what the next step will be.

Franz: Yes.

Jan: So, you're going to talk to your team and get feedback from them and I'm going to contact the suppliers and ask them to come up with some new designs, right?

Franz: That's right, yes. Er… Let's meet again, shall we say, next month?

Jan: Right, what date would suit you?

Franz: Well, I'm free most days …

Unit 25 A2

Sue: Extension 279, can I help you?

Mike: Ah, hi, Sue, it's Mike.

Sue: Mike, hello!

Mike: Er…listen, you're doing the agenda for the meeting on the 15th, aren't you?

Sue: Mhm, yeah, I've just printed it out. Do you want me to fax you a copy?

Mike: Ah…n…no. Er…the thing is there are a few changes. Do you…do you mind doing it again?

Sue: No, that's OK. What are the changes?

Mike: Right, well, item 4…er…that was going to be Julie and Nancy's presentation. Well, now Julie's just called to say there's been a …some sort of hold up in production development. So we're going to postpone that till February. So can you delete item 4, please?

Sue: Mmm, yeah, and renumber the rest. Sure.

Mike: Ah, now…oh…sorry, no. Er…there are a few more changes. Now, Carlo isn't going to be coming to the meeting. That presentation…er…it's going to be given by…er…Andrea Rossi.

Sue: A N D R E A R O double S I ?

Mike: Yeah. A…and one more change. Meeting Room 5 is being redecorated. So…er…one of the teams will have to meet in the coffee room.

Sue: Oh, that's OK. And…er…does that mean all the times after Item 3 can be brought forward by half an hour?

Mike: Ah, yeah, that's right. Er…and we'll have coffee 10:30, lunch at ten to two.

Sue: Oh, that's fine. OK, Mike, I'll redo this and send you a copy to check before I copy it to all the other people. Will there still be 13 for lunch?

Mike: Er…yeah, I think so.

Sue: All right.

Mike: Thank you, Sue.

Unit 25 B1

Chair: Good morning, everyone. Welcome.

Everyone: Good morning …

Chair: Right. First of all, if you have a mobile phone, could you please turn it off?

Everyone: All right …

Chair: Right, has everyone got a copy of the agenda?

Everyone: Yes, yes …

Chair: All right. Now, the first item on the agenda is the discussion on the …

Chair: … Right, so, thank you Mr White. Er…does anyone have any questions before we move on?

Mr Harris: Yes, could I ask a question, please?

Chair: Mr Harris?

Mr Harris: Mr White, can you give us any idea of when the planning stage will be finished?

Mr Harris: Not till after Christmas, I'm afraid.

Ms Lewis: Oh…um…er…could I just say something?

Chair: Ms Lewis?

Ms Lewis: If it isn't finished till after Christmas, that w…that probably means that we'll all be kept waiting till the middle or even the end of January. By then our competitors will have their new products on the market and we …

Mr Harris: Sorry, c...could I interrupt for a moment?
Ms Lewis: Yeah.
Mr Harris: I can promise that everything will be ready on January 1st.
Chair: All right, Ms Lewis?
Ms Lewis: Thank you, I just wanted to be sure.
Chair: Thank you everyone. Now, shall we move on to the next point?
Everyone: Yes, yes . . .
Chair: Well, we're nearly out of time. Can we come to a conclusion? Is there any other business?
Everyone: No, I don't think so, no . . .
Chair: Well, thank you very much, everyone. We'll meet again on the 11th of next month at 2 o'clock.
Everyone: Great, OK, fine . . .

Unit 26 B1

Kevin: . . . so that's our proposal. And now we can start work...er...next month if you're agreeable.
Donna: Well, the thing is we actually need to get it installed by the end of this month. The ventilation system we have now is so noisy!
Kevin: Mm...ours is totally silent! Er...well, we might be able to do it this month, but then we would have to do the work during normal office hours.
Donna: Well, that's not going to work at all, is it? Couldn't you install it at night so as not to disrupt the office?
Kevin: Well, we could do that, er...but not this month, I'm afraid. Our installation team could fit in a Saturday if you can close the office on a Saturday. But they would have to be paid overtime for that, so of course that would increase the cost.
Donna: Well, that's going to be difficult, isn't it, because we normally work on Saturdays. Well, I mean, maybe the last Saturday of the month might be a possibility.
Kevin: Let me just check that, that's the...the...um...27th. Oh, yes, our team are available then. Er...would you be prepared to split the extra labour costs with us?
Donna: Well, I suppose that sounds reasonable. Well, all right, all right, I'll...I'll agree to that. Now th...the other thing is we have to decide is about maintenance.
Kevin: Oh, yes, that's right.
Donna: I mean, we would expect you to provide free maintenance for at least the first 12 months.
Kevin: Certainly. Our engineer will come to you within 24 hours to fix anything, you know, that might go wrong. Well, that's of course automatically included.
Donna: Oh, well, good, all right. But what about after that?
Kevin: Well, we have a service contract. You see, you pay so much a year for the same service. Well, that...it does include a...a twice-yearly regular visit to check the whole system. I've got the prices here, look.
Donna: Well, that seems completely unnecessary to me. Can't you provide the same service without the twice-yearly visit for less?
Kevin: Ah, well, that's difficult. A...actually not really advisable. It's always better to find faults before they happen, ra...rather than wait until things go wrong.
Donna: Oh yeah, well, how often do you expect your systems to break down then?
Kevin: Er...well, actually they...they're extremely reliable. Er...look, all right, what if we ask you to pay the cost of our engineer's time if there is a problem to fix? But we will pay for any spare parts during the year following the first 12 months. Well, that's fair, isn't it?
Donna: Yes. All right. So, we seem to be agreed that for a total price, including installation, we will pay you . . .

Unit 27 A2

Charles Cotton: Relationships are...are very important in...er...in ...in Asia generally. You need to have a number of meetings really to, you know, lay the ground work, to get to know each other, to get to know each other's companies and to build trust. I think that that's important. I think, in an American context...um...the trust is much more represented by the...er...the nature of the companies that you represent, rather than the individual trust between the people who are negotiating the particular contract that's...er...in place. That's also important that the...that the personalities don't clash, but...er...er...people are generally minded to want to get to a conclusion much more quickly in...in America. It's a rather slower process in...in Asia...um...and a contract which in America perhaps could be drawn up, negotiated, signed, sealed and delivered in two weeks, could take you two months or more in...in Asia with a...a 'decency period' between each meeting and a...a time for reflection and so on.

Unit 27 A3

Peter Callaghan: In Australia what you do is you just sort of say, 'Well, this is what I would like to achieve, these are the points I think we've got to make some compromises on.' The other party would say the same thing. You'd tick off the ones where you've got agreement and then you'd start to hammer out some sort of compromise on the ones that you are in disagreement. Whereas here...ah...you'd...you'd outline perhaps what you want or what you'd like to achieve. Er...and the first meeting it would appear that none of it's contentious, but clearly it would be, but you...it'd take several meetings and several rounds of negotiation. Because I think...um...in Europe there's a lot more...there's a lots...lots...much greater awareness of the 'hidden agenda'. So you...you've really got to spend a lot of time...um...explaining what you'd like and why you want it and, you know, trying to understand the other person's point of view. And it might take weeks, whereas in Australia you'd do that in a day.

The personal dangers to reputation, to position are a lot greater in Europe, 'face'...um...is a lot greater here. But if you get something wrong, you lose your face a lot...it's a bit like Japan. Japan is, you know, they talk about it there. Europe is much the same. It...you have to be...o...in my experience you have to be very careful about committing to things. Whereas in Australia you could negotiate with something and you might innocently get something wrong and you'd think, 'Well, hang on, I'm going to be disadvantaged by this.' In Australia you'd just go back to the other party and say, 'Look, I don't agree now, I want to change this.' And you could start again. Whereas I think in Europe you have to be a lot...people are a lot more careful about before they commit. They...they want to understand in detail...um...what the implications are for them.

Whereas Japanese are pretty straight to negotiate with. They...they will take their time. Um...and they are like the Europeans, they...they don't want to make a mistake. But once they commit they are incredibly diligent, and very committed to a project. Often when a European or an Anglo-Saxon would have given up, the Japanese will keep going. They'll want to make a success of it once they've committed.

Unit 29 A2

Secretary: Madame Fulbert is here, Bob.

Bob Campbell: Thank you. Hello, Madame Fulbert, welcome to Canada!

Corinne Fulbert: Mr Campbell. I'm so sorry to be late.

    Bob: That's all right. I've had plenty to get on with. Was your plane delayed?

Corinne: No, I arrived last night, actually. The flight was fine, we landed on time at 8pm, and I'm staying at the Dominion.

    Bob: Oh, very nice! I suppose they forgot to give you a wake-up call?

Corinne: No, I left the hotel at 9 o'clock. But my taxi's had…had a flat tyre. And the driver's spare tyre was flat, too. So it took an hour to get it fixed. Then the traffic was really bad on the freeway, so that's why I'm so late.

    Bob: Oh, well, never mind, you're here now. Would you like to freshen up?

Corinne: No, I'm fine, thank you. But some coffee would be nice.

    Bob: Certainly, how would you like it?

Corinne: Strong and black, please.

    Bob: All right. By the way, I've booked lunch for 12:30. Do you like Chinese food, Madame Fulbert?

Corinne: Yes, I do, actually. And please call me Corinne.

    Bob: All right. And I'm Bob.

Corinne: Bob, before I forget, I've brought you a small gift from Pa…from France.

    Bob: Oh, you shouldn't have! Well, that's very kind of you. *[He unwraps it.]*

Corinne: It's a CD-Rom of paintings in the Louvre Museum in Paris.

    Bob: Oh, how nice! Ohh, I think it's the same one my daughter brought back for me when she went there.

Corinne: Oh, OK, well, don't worry, give it back to me and I will change it for another one. I'll send it back to you.

    Bob: Oh, that's … Oh, sorry, I…I shouldn't have …

Corinne: Don't worry, don't worry, I can easily change it …

Unit 29 A3

Corinne: Hello, Bob. It's really nice to see you again.

    Bob: And it's good to see you, Corinne, how are you?

Corinne: Very well. Did you have a good journey?

    Bob: Oh, yes, thanks. Er…it was fine.

Corinne: Er…can I take your coat?

    Bob: Oh, yes, please. I'll just put my scarf in the sleeve.

Corinne: And do you need to freshen up?

    Bob: Yes, please. Could I use your bathroom?

Corinne: Yes, it's …

Corinne: … Do sit down.

    Bob: Thanks.

Corinne: Now, would you like something to drink?

    Bob: I'd love a coffee, please. Black, no sugar.

Corinne: Fine. I've booked lunch for 1 o'clock. Is that OK?

    Bob: Oh, yes. That's great.

Corinne: Are you booked into a hotel tonight?

    Bob: Yes, I'm staying at the one you recommended, the Cambridge.

Corinne: Oh, yes, that's really nice. Oh, er…would you like me to show you around the factory?

    Bob: Oh, I certainly would, that would be really interesting.

Corinne: All right. Let's do that when we've finished our coffee.

    Bob: Mhm.

Corinne: And would you like Tim to look after your bag till later?

    Bob: Oh yes, th…that's a good idea, yeah. I just need to get a something out of here first. Here we are. This is for you.

Corinne: Oh, what is it?

    Bob: Well, just a little gift from Canada. I hope you like it.

Corinne: Oh, thank you very much indeed, it's really kind of you. *[She unwraps it.]*

    Bob: You're very welcome.

Corinne: Oh! A bottle of Canadian wine. How nice!

Unit 30 A2

1

Announcement: Flight GA 737 will be delayed until 9:30 due to the late arrival of the incoming aircraft.

    Jim: Oh, no! That's us.

Emma: Oh, what's the time now?

    Jim: Er…8 o'clock.

Emma: Oh, dear.

    Jim: What are you reading?

Emma: This.

    Jim: Oh, er…mm…I…er…I…I don't know that writer.

Emma: She's good.

    Jim: Oh.

Emma: Do you…er…do you like reading?

    Jim: I don't have much time for it.

Emma: Oh.

    Jim: Hmm.

Emma: I've got this week's Time Magazine. Would you like to look at that?

    Jim: OK. Yeah, thanks. It's…er…it's a pity we …

Emma: What?

    Jim: Nothing.

2

Announcement: Flight GA 737 will be delayed until 9:30 due to the late arrival of the incoming aircraft.

    Jim: Oh, no! that's us.

Emma: Oh! What's the time now?

    Jim: 8 o'clock.

Emma: Oh, dear.

    Jim: What are you reading?

Emma: Oh, er…this. I…it's Barbara Vine's latest.

    Jim: Barbara Vine. I…is she good?

Emma: Yes, she's excellent.

    Jim: Right, well…er…what sort of…er…what sort of books does she write?

Emma: Well, well, they're thrillers but they're a bit unusual.

    Jim: Right, er…in what…in what way are they unusual?

Emma: Well, the characters are always a bit strange.

    Jim: Strange?

Emma: Yeah. They're mostly losers who get involved in murders.

    Jim: That sounds a bit depressing!

Emma: Well, in a way, but the stories are so well-told that you just want to keep on reading.

    Jim: Oh, I see, right.

Emma: What about you? Do you enjoy reading?

    Jim: W…I…I don't have much time for it, I'm afraid.

Emma: Oh, that's a shame. But when you do have time, what do you like to read?

    Jim: Well, you know, same as you, I…I like thrillers.

Emma: Oh! What writers do you like?

    Jim: Oh, let me think. Aah, the last one I read I think was by …

Unit 30 C2

    Man: … agree with you. Did you read about the new electric car in the paper today?

Woman: Yes.

    Man: What do you think of it?

Woman: It sounds like a really good idea. The thing is, I just wonder whether it really …

    Man: … before. Er…is everything all right with your hotel?

Woman: Not really.

    Man: Oh, I'm sorry to hear that. Well, what's the problem exactly?

Woman: Well, I asked for a quiet room but the only room they had is right over the garage . . .

Man: . . . went there last year. Have you been away on holiday this year?
Woman: Yes.
Man: Er…did you go somewhere nice?
Woman: Yes, Spain.
Man: Oh, really, and what part of Spain did you go to?
Woman: Well, we hadn't really planned where exactly we'd go but . . .

Man: . . . sounds like a good idea to me. Um…have you seen any good movies lately?
Woman: Yes.
Man: Oh, which one did you see last? I mean, w…would you recommend it?
Woman: The last one was the new James Bond film. I don't think I'd really recommend it because he had a really funny . . .

Man: . . . rather fond of music myself. What kind of music do you like?
Woman: Classical.
Man: Oh, and who is your favourite composer?
Woman: Well, it depends on my mood. When I want to relax I love listening to Schubert, especially . . .

Man: . . . perhaps I'll try that restaurant next week. Er…what do you like to do in your spare time?
Woman: I like to read.
Man: Oh, really. And who is your favourite writer?
Woman: I love reading thrillers, and my favourite author is Barbara Vine, she just has a way with words . . .

Man: . . . will you have any time to see the city?
Woman: Yes.
Man: Oh, good. Do you know what you want to go and see?
Woman: Not really. Where would you recommend?
Man: Well, I have to say, there's a brilliant art museum and there's a very nice . . .

Unit 31 A2

Hans: Can I invite you to have dinner with us this evening, Astrid?
Astrid: Ah, that would be nice. Thank you.
Hans: What kind of food do you like?
Astrid: Oh, I don't mind. I like all kinds of food.
Hans: Oh, well, there are plenty of places to choose from then!
Astrid: Uhuh, and where do you recommend?
Hans: Well, the Golden Dragon is very nice. Their food is always good – freshly prepared and the people are very friendly.
Astrid: And w…what kind of food do they have there?
Hans: It's Chinese. Would that be OK?
Astrid: Well, w…what are the other choices?
Hans: Lorenzo's is a nice place because it's right beside the lake. It's going to be a warm evening, so we could sit outside if we book a table on the terrace.
Astrid: And is that…is that Italian?
Hans: Yes. Their seafood is very good. Or you could have a pizza if you prefer. They do lovely pizzas – just like the ones you get in Italy.
Astrid: Sounds nice.
Hans: You can sit outside at the Golden Dragon, too. Or there's Le Bistro. That's a very nice French place. Very central. They don't have an outdoor area, though.
Astrid: Mm, I like French food.
Hans: Yes, their speciality is free-range meat – and they have organic vegetables. It's quite small but if we book, I think we can get a table for five people.
Astrid: But, you know, I actually feel like eating outdoors.

Hans: All right. In that case it's a choice between the Chinese and the Italian.
Astrid: Are they both easy to get to, do you think?
Hans: The Golden Dragon is in the centre. Lorenzo's is outside town. I could collect you from your hotel in my car and we could drive there. Easier for me to park there, too. Er…we can meet the others there.
Astrid: All right. We go there!
Hans: 8 o'clock?
Astrid: Yah!
Hans: I'll pick you up at 7:45, then. But first I'll call them and book a table.

Unit 32 A2

Leo: Excuse me. Can you tell me how to get to Seaport Village, please?
Woman: Seaport Village? Sure. OK, you're here at the Broadway Pier.
Leo: Right.
Woman: To get to Seaport Village you just keep walking south down Harbor Drive.
Leo: Right.
Woman: You go past Tuna Harbor and you'll get to Seaport Village. It's very easy to find.
Leo: Oh right, thank you very much.
Woman: Uhuh.

Leo: Er…excuse me.
Man: Yes.
Leo: Can you tell me how to get to the Hyatt Regency Hotel?
Man: Yes, no problem. Just look up! It's…see down there, the tallest building down there, that's the Hyatt Regency.
Leo: Oh, right, OK.
Man: So, walk up Kettner Boulevard until you get to Harbor Drive, then make a right and just keep looking up, you'll see which one it is, it's on the right.
Leo: Oh, OK, thank you very much.
Man: You're most welcome.

Leo: Hi.
Woman: Hi.
Leo: Hi, can you tell me how to get to the Historic Gaslamp Quarter?
Woman: Oh, sure. Are you walking?
Leo: Yeah.
Woman: OK. Well, first you go up Harbor Drive until you get to Market Street.
Leo: Right.
Woman: OK, then you cross over the railroad tracks on Market Street and keep going until you reach Fifth Avenue, and then you're almost there. You just have to go up Fifth Avenue till you get to Broadway.
Leo: OK, thank you!
Woman: You're welcome.

Leo: Er…excuse me.
Man: Yes.
Leo: Can you tell me the quickest way to get to the Convention Center from here?
Man: Well, the quickest way is to take the Trolley.
Leo: Oh, right.
Man: Yeah, it stops near there so i…it'll take you most of the way.
Leo: OK.
Man: Yeah, get off across from the Marriott Hotel on Harbor Drive.
Leo: Right.
Man: And the Convention Center…mm…is just a short walk down Harbor Drive from there.
Leo: Oh, great, thanks very much.

Leo: Hi.

Woman: Oh, hello.

Leo: Hi, can you tell me how to get to a restaurant? It's called Anthony's Star of the Sea Room a…and I'd like to walk there.

Woman: Oh…er…oh, sure, it's…um…oh, it's on North Harbor Drive.

Leo: Oh, right.

Woman: So, you just walk north along the harbor past the piers. Um…it…it's right on the waterfront – oh, at…at the end of Ash Street.

Leo: OK.

Woman: It's a…It's a very nice restaurant. Oh, do you have a reservation?

Leo: Yeah, yes, I do, I'm meeting some people there actually.

Woman: Oh, good, well, enjoy the seafood!

Leo: Thank you very much!

Leo: Excuse me, how do I get from here to the Hotel del Coronado.

Man: The Del?

Leo: Yes.

Woman: Ah, well, if you walk down along the harbor until you get to the Broadway Pier, you can hop on the ferry there.

Leo: OK.

Man: Yeah, it'll take you to Coronado, but then i…it's quite a walk to the Del from the terminal at the other end. My advice is: you get a taxi from there. Just ask the driver to take you to the Del. It's just a few minutes by cab.

Leo: OK, thanks very much, bye.

Man: No problem, bye-bye.

Unit 33 A2

Mr Wong: Good evening, my name's Wong. I have a room booked for tonight.

Receptionist: Oh, good evening, Mr Wong. Um…I'll just check for you on the computer, won't be a minute … Ah, yes, here we are. And you're staying with us for three nights, is that right?

Mr Wong: Yes. Do you have a room with a balcony?

Receptionist: Oh, I'm afraid none of our rooms have balconies, Mr Wong.

Mr Wong: Well, I'd like a room that doesn't overlook the street, please.

Receptionist: Oh, yes, certainly, we can arrange that for you. Um…here, room 808 overlooks the park at the back of the hotel. And it's also got a very nice view of the city.

Mr Wong: That sounds fine.

Receptionist: And how would you like to pay for your room?

Mr Wong: I'm going to pay by Visa. Here's my card.

Receptionist: Oh, thank you very much, that'll do nicely. I'll just take an imprint and then …

Receptionist: Good morning, Mme Duval. How may I help you?

Mme Duval: Well, I would like to extend my stay for another night if I can.

Receptionist: Yes, I think that'll be all right. Let me just check the computer … Ah, you're in Room 810, is that right?

Mme Duval: Yes, 810. Is there a problem?

Receptionist: N…no, not really. It's just that Room 810 is already booked.

Mme Duval: I don't mind moving to a different room if necessary.

Receptionist: No, that's not necessary. I'll just alter this other booking to Room 812. You can stay in Room 810. Just one more night, you said?

Mme Duval: That's right. Thanks very much.

Receptionist: Good evening, Mr Stein.

Mr Stein: Good evening. I'm leaving the hotel very early tomorrow. Can I check out and pay my bill in the morning?

Receptionist: Um…what time are you leaving?

Mr Stein: At 5 o'clock. My flight leaves at 8 o'clock.

Receptionist: Well, it would be best if you could settle your bill tonight.

Mr Stein: All right. Er…what time?

Receptionist: Well, any time before midnight is fine, Mr Stein.

Mr Stein: Oh, and…er…could you book me a taxi to the airport, please?

Receptionist: Certainly. For 5 o'clock?

Unit 34 A2

Host: Hello?

Jeremy Allen: Hello. This is…er…Jeremy Allen. I'm…er…I'm afraid I won't be on the flight tomorrow morning. So please, you know, don't come and pick me up from the airport. I thin…I…I got held up on the way to the airport here and…er…basically by the time I got here there were no seats left and … The airline had oversold the seats and by the time I got there, there were no seats left, so I've … I don't know what to do. I mean, w…what do you think I should do?

Host: Well, . . .

Host: Hello?

Tina Barnes: Hello, this is Tina Barnes.

Host: Oh, hi, Tina.

Tina: I…I've got this…I've got a bit of a problem. I'm…um…I'm leaving my hotel early tomorrow and I have to pay my bill this evening. Well, I gave them my credit card but for some reason my bank's computer won't authorize the payment.

Host: Oh, dear. Um . . .

Tina: I mean, it's a company card, so I…I can't understand it. I mean, the…you see, the trouble is, I don't actually have enough cash to pay the bill.

Host: OK . . .

Tina: So, what do you think I should do?

Host: Well, . . .

Host: Hello?

Helmut Schranz: Hello. This is Helmut Schranz.

Host: Oh, Helmut, hi. How are you?

Helmut: I…I wonder if you can help me. I'm here at the airport and my flight leaves in an hour. The problem is my suitcase has gone missing. I put it in the trunk of the taxi and when we got here I paid the driver. But my suitcase had gone.

Host: Oh, that's unfortunate. Um . . .

Helmut: There was another one the same colour on the sidewalk. I…I think someone must have got mine and I've got his. I didn't have my name on mine, and there's no name on this one. What do you think I should do?

Host: OK. Um…well, . . .

Host: Hello?

Laura Davis: Oh, hello, hi, er…this is Laura – Laura Davis.

Host: Oh, hi.

Laura: Um…um…I'm in a spot of trouble. I…I just went to the bank to change some traveller's cheques into cash, and…but when I opened my bag I found that my wallet wasn't there. Now, either someone has taken my wallet from my bag or I left it at home and I didn't bring it with me. So, well I…I just don't know what to do. I mean, I need to … Ohh! Oh, here's my wallet. Oh, no! It's completely empty – no credit cards, no cash, no traveller's cheques. Ohh, what am I going to do?

Host: Oh dear, well, um . . .

Host: Hello?

Jeremy Allen: Hello, er…this is Jeremy Allen again . . .

Host: Oh, hi.

Jeremy: Yeah, hi. I've got some good news and some bad news. What…what do you want to hear first?

Host: Er…tell me the good news.

Jeremy: Well, er…there was an early morning flight with another airline, so I managed to get a seat on that. Er…so, now I'm, you know, here at the hotel. But I've got a bit of a problem.

Host: All right, what is the bad news?

Jeremy: They don't seem to have a record of my reservation – I…the booking must have been automatically cancelled or something.

Host: Which hotel are you at?

Jeremy: Er…the Royal Prince.

Host: The Royal Prince or the Royal Princess?

Jeremy: Oh, don't tell me there's a Royal Princess Hotel as well?

Host: Yes, but it's two hours' drive from the Royal Prince.

Jeremy: Oh, right, well, mm…what do you think I should do?

Host: Well, . . .

Unit 34 A3

Jeremy: . . . there were no seats left, so I've . . . I don't know what to do. I mean, w…what do you think I should do?

Host: Well, the best thing to do is to see if you can get a seat on another airline. There might be a later flight tonight, or a flight tomorrow morning.

Tina: . . . I don't have actually enough cash to pay the bill.

Host: OK . . .

Tina: So, what do you think I should do?

Host: Well, the only thing to do is…er…for us to pay for your room and you can pay us back later. I could probably authorize payment over the phone. I'll give them my credit card number and they'll charge it to me.

Helmut: . . . I didn't have my name on mine, and there's no name on this one. What do you think I should do?

Host: OK. Um…well, I think you should go to the Airport Information desk and report this to them and leave the case with them. With any luck the other person will find out that he's taken the wrong case and get in touch with Airport Information, too. You should tell your airline, too a…and ask them to send your case on when it's found. Call me again before you leave to tell me what's happened. I…I can chase the Airport people for you if necessary.

Helmut: Thanks.

Laura: . . . it's completely empty – no credit cards, no cash, no traveller's cheques. Ohh, what am I going to do?

Host: Oh, dear, well, um…look, the first thing to do i…is go to the main police station to report the theft. I'll get in my car now and meet you there. Then I can help you make the report to the police and lend you some money.

Laura: Oh, thank you!

Jeremy: . . . don't tell me there's a Royal Princess Hotel as well?

Host: Yes, but it's two hours' drive from the Royal Prince.

Jeremy: Oh, right, well, mm…what do you think I should do?

Host: Well, there's no point in driving all that way. So, first of all, find out if the Royal Prince has a nice room free. If they have, you could stay there.

Jeremy: Yeah, but they haven't got a room. I…I asked them already.

Host: OK, then…er . . . You'd better call the Royal Princess before you set off to make sure they do have a room for you.

Jeremy: Er…OK. Er…yeah, well, I'll do what you suggest. Thanks for the advice.

Unit 35 A2

Toby Nicol: easyJet as a company was officially incorporated in March 1995 by our then and current chairman Stelios Haji-Ioannou. Initially, easyJet was conceptualized as an airline to carry people business class out of Athens to various business destinations around the world. However, on his…the…Stelios's tours around the world in order to look at business models for airlines he stumbled across a number of very different concepts, which essentially involved taking all of the costs and the frills out of the business. And that's essentially where easyJet was formed. easyJet now is a no frills low cost airline, we have 20 aircraft flying on a total of 31 routes purely within Europe. The airline …er…f…flew its first flight in November 1995, er…which was to Glasgow, shortly followed by Edinburgh. In the last five years therefore we've expanded tremendously and it was in mid-November 2000 that easyJet finally floated on the London stock market and at the time the airline was valuated (valued) at just short of £800 million, which is a fair achievement in just five years.

It was in 1998 that Stelios decided to set up other companies. The…the next venture which was announced and introduced was…er…easyEverything, a chain of Internet cafés, which opened in London in the summer of 1999. And to date there's probably twenty Internet cafés around the world, including what is now the largest Internet…largest Internet café in the world, which is the opening of easyEverything in Times Square in New York. Further ventures to come out of the easyGroup, as the holding company is called, easyRentacar, the world's first Internet-only car rental company. And again, this company is dedicated to reducing costs and taking frills out of it…out of its business. Er…for example, there's only one kind of car which is used, in order to keep costs low. Most recently, there's another venture called easyValue.com. This is essentially a robot piece of software which goes into…er…individual companies' websites in order to extract the…the best prices for things. So you could for example ask for a flight from London to Belfast, it would go and analyse websites for a number of airlines and come back to you with the best price.

Unit 35 A3

Toby: The structure of easyJet and the other easy companies is very similar. All of them were built on a very, very flat management structure, where there's the chairman, Stelios Haji-Ioannou, and each of those that then got a…a…a chief executive and a number of board directors, and below that you're into the…the main management of…of the airline. But unlike other companies, the easy companies are not restricted by endless layers of bureaucracy. We have…it's a very, very efficient company. We have a paperless office system which…which reduces the need for…um…excess frills within the organization. There's very, very few photocopiers or computer printers here, and one of the extensions of that it's very, very easy to communicate both internally within the company, and externally.

We're still based in a…a bright orange converted shed near the main taxi-way at Luton Airport, it's called 'easyLand', it's all open-plan, everybody dresses casually, there's no secretaries, there's no private offices, people come and go as…as they please. And essentially taking frills and complexity out of the business is what easyJet is all about. Everything we can do we do in order to minimize cost, and we have an absolute commitment in order to taking cost out of the business and therefore continuing to offer low fares to…to customers.

Unit 36 A1

1

Man: OK, when this red light comes on, that means the batteries need replacing.

Woman: Oh, I see.

Man: So, the first thing you have to do is…er…you have to turn it over, and you have to take out the old ones. Now it's this little compartment here, you need to slide that aside gently and flip it up . . .

Woman: Oh, right.

Man: So we take the old batteries out. Now these ones, they're rechargeable so I can use them again later. Then you get your two new ones and you have to insert them like this. Now make sure that the end of each battery with the minus sign is touching the little springs. If you get it the wrong way round, they won't work. . . . There, OK. So, that's all there is to it.

Woman: Oh, that's brilliant.

Man: Any questions?

Woman: No.

2

Woman: . . . when you press this little button . . .

Man: Yeah.

Woman: There we are . . .

Man: Oh, right.

Woman: The hands go round to show the time the alarm's set for. There we are, it's set.

Man: I see.

Woman: Then you can reset the alarm time by pulling the button out and turning the hands to the time you want. And then you push the button back in. There we are! And now the hands automatically go back to the time now.

Man: Oh, right.

Woman: When the alarm goes off it makes this noise . . . *[musical alarm plays]*

Man: Haha!

Woman: Haha! There we are, it's gone back now to the time now.

Man: Oh, brilliant!

Woman: Whatever you do, if you want to set the alarm, press the button *in* first and then you pull the button out to reset the alarm. If you pull the button out without pressing it first, you'll reset the time now, which you obviously, you don't want to do.

Man: Right, oh, brilliant. Thanks very much.

3

Man: OK, so when you press the ON button it makes this sound. *[sound]* Right! And you can adjust the volume by pushing this little lever here.

Woman: Yeah.

Man: And then you press the keys to make a calculation. Er…for example:

Calculator: '154 point 68 divided by 200'

Man: Then I press the EQUALS button.

Calculator: 'Equals O point 7734'

Man: And also, if I turn it upside down, it says 'Hello'.

Woman: Haha.

Man: And you can make the voice say the result again by pressing the REPEAT button. Like this:

Calculator: 'O point 7734'

Man: Right, but the important thing is not to turn the volume to OFF, otherwise you don't hear the voice. OK?

Woman: Yeah, of course, yeah.

Man: So, now you try doing it.

Woman: Yeah, OK, have a go.

4

Woman: . . . if the ink runs out, it's easy to replace the cartridge. First, you unscrew the bottom off the pen . . .

Man: Yeah.

Woman: And you'll see the old cartridge attached to the top. Look, it's empty as you can see.

Man: Oh, yeah.

Woman: Then, you pull it off and get a new cartridge and push it on like that – you can feel a little click as it goes in.

Man: OK.

Woman: Now, make sure you push it firmly, otherwise the ink may leak out. Then screw the bottom back on and it should work . . . Yes, it does.

Man: Great!

Woman: There you are. Good as new.

Unit 36 B1

Man: I…I want to use the overhead projector for my presentation. Could you show me how to use it?

Woman: OK, yeah, let me show you. Just watch what I do. I…I'll talk you through the procedure.

Man: OK, yeah, thanks.

Woman: Right, well. First of all, you put the OHP on the table here, about 2 metres from the wall or the screen. Er…do you have a screen?

Man: Er…no. I…I thought I'd just use the wall.

Woman: Oh, er…well, a screen's better, but I suppose this wall will be all right. It is sort of white. Anyway, let's try it. So, the next thing you have to do is press these buttons in and lift this part up until it snaps into place.

Man: OK, yeah.

Woman: And then turn it round so the head is facing towards the screen, I mean wall, and now we can plug it in.

Man: Right, and you switch it on?

Woman: Yeah. Then I press the switch here on the front . . .

Man: Right.

Woman: There! And the light should come on.

Man: Right, OK.

Woman: Yeah, there we are. So, you just place your transparency here on the glass.

Man: OK, there, oh!

Woman: Oh, no! No, the other way up.

Man: Right, of course.

Woman: That's right, yeah. And to raise or lower the image you move this flap up or down . . . There, that's better.

Man: Right, OK.

Woman: And finally, to focus the image you turn this wheel to make it sharp . . . That's . . . There we are, that's not too bad.

Man: Oh, that's great, yeah. OK, thanks!

Woman: Oh, one more thing: whatever you do, don't keep switching it on and off. I'm going to switch it off now. Now, you should leave it switched on, with a piece of paper over the glass

Man: Right, I…er…I don't understand why you have to leave it on.

Woman: Well, the reason why you have to do that is that you don't want the bulb to fail. If it does, you'll have to replace the bulb, which will be very hot and you may not have a spare anyway. So that's about it. Any questions?

Man: Erm…no, that…that all seems all very clear. Well, thank you very much.

Woman: You're welcome. Oh, and I really do think you need to get a screen, by the way. The picture would be much brighter than on that wall, you know.

Man: Oh, OK. Well, um…I'll…I'll ask Jim if he's got one.

Woman: Oh, good idea! And make sure he shows you how to put it up!

Man: Haha! I will! Thanks again.

Unit 37 A1

Narrator: Joost, how did it all start?

Joost Meijerink: It all started…um…with the original Flexifoil kite. It's in here, in this catalogue actually. This…this is the kite that really started it all. The original six-foot Power Kite. That's how the company started, with that product only.

The…the two types of products we have at the moment are the…the…the leisure…the recreational products for people that enjoy…um…flying a powerful kite that, you know, enjoy playing with the wind, you know, playing with the elements. And then the other type of product it's the…the extreme sport products…err…like the kite surf…er…products we manufacture.

Narrator: How long does it take to produce a kite?

Joost: From concept to…um…finished on-the-shelf product is…is…is…is…a…a…l…long time goes by. I mean…er…designing a project from concept to getting it on the shelf is usually…it usually takes about a year to eighteen months at least. Um…it starts with an idea, and then we…we…we make some prototypes, er…'proof-of-concept' prototypes, then we start developing that idea. Er…see if we can actually make it into a useful product and that is usually where all the time goes, that's where most of the time goes. And…um…as soon as we think we have a product which is actually usable for what we want to use it for, er…we'll produce a limited quantity for our testers, which are basically our sponsored riders. Those people are…are…are the sort of people we use at the moment to test our products. And that's quite a lengthy process as well because all these tests kites go out, they go out with e…evaluation forms which have to be filled in and then changes have to be made. So then we've got to translate that…that…that kite…er…into a product that can actually be manufactured. Now, once we've done that, we…we…we des…we start applying graphics and colours and all the marketing spiel to it, and then …er…we put it into production.

Narrator: And you have an overseas manufacturing partner to do that. What happens in that part of the process?

Joost: First of all, we have a working prototype, or working sample. Usually the whole…at the moment, especially, everything is designed on a computer. So they get all the computer files for the patterns, everything delivered on disk or CD. And…and we tell them which materials we want to use, what colours we want to use. With a kite material there's many…er…different things you have to think about when you spec a material. First of all, it's got to be light, it's got to be airtight, it's got to be UV-resistant. And especially with these new water-…er…based products, the water…er…the material should not absorb any water, it should dry quickly, it should shed the water quickly.

Narrator: What happens after you've checked all the details and the manufacturer has gone ahead and actually produced the kites?

Joost: We find the easiest way to stick the whole lot in a big container, ship it here and distribute from here. In the UK we sell…supply most shops direct from…er…this building here, we … And we have a…a sub-distributor in…in…in the…um…the UK, which takes care of…of some shops, but most shops we supply direct from here. Then we try and have distributors in…in most other major countries and then we supply the distributors from here and they distribute to the shops. It's a…it's a very simple distribution system.

And as I said, usually from…from idea to…to…to product on the shelf is at least eighteen months. It's…it's a long process.

Unit 37 B2

Woman: First, you choose the e-mail program on your computer and click 'New Message'.

Man: All right.

Woman: OK? Well, then you start typing the name of the recipient. The program remembers the name and completes the e-mail address. Well, if not, you look up the name in the address book or contacts list. OK? Well, if you want other people to get copies of the same message, you send them 'CCs', which are copies of the message. OK? Well, then you press Return on the keyboard and then you type the subject of the message. Now, there's no need to put the date because that goes in automatically when you send the message, together with the time. OK?

Man: Oh, yeah, oh, OK.

Woman: Yeah? OK. Well, then you press Return again and start writing the message. Now, if you make a mistake, you just press Backspace to delete the previous letter or word and then type it again correctly.

Man: Right.

Woman: All right? OK. Now, when you've finished, you read the whole message through to make sure it looks right and contains the right information. Now, if you decide you want to change sentences around, you can copy sentences and paste them in other places.

Man: And…er…er…how about spelling and punctuation, er…that can be corrected automatically, can't it?

Woman: Well, yes. Well, you can run your spell checker and that may bring up some mis-typings and things like that. But it definitely won't catch them all, so you must read it through to check your spelling, too. And check your punctuation at the same time. Now, if you notice a misspelt word, or if you want to change a word or something like that, double-click on the word and type the new word over it.

Man: Fine. That's easy.

Woman: Hmhm. And then it's ready to send. You just click on 'Send' and it'll go off when you next go Online. And the other person will find your message in their Inbox when they next go Online to get their messages.

Man: Right. Well, that sounds much easier than handwriting a message and faxing it.

Woman: I know, sure it does, well, it's …

Unit 38 B1

Maria: Excuse me, sir, have you seen this product before?

Customer: No, I haven't .

Maria: Well, it's called the Pocket Reader. Would you like a quick demonstration to see you how it works?

Customer: All right.

Maria: May I use your newspaper?

Customer: Yes, here you are.

Maria: Thank you. OK, now, first I press this little button to switch it on and then I move it across the top of the article like this …

Maria: …and you can read the sentences I've scanned here in the little window.

Customer: Ohh!

Woman: Now you try with the next paragraph.

Customer: Oh, yes! Yes, very impressive. This is the kind of thing my customers might go for.

Maria: What they'll most appreciate is that it can be used anywhere – away from the office, their computer. And as you just saw, it's easy to use and it's easy to give your customers a quick demonstration – and then ask them to try it for themselves.

Customer: Well!

Woman: It takes no time to learn how to use.

Customer: Yes.

Maria: And it's totally reliable – we do have a no quibble return policy, but so far nobody has sent one back to us with any fault. So you won't have to worry about providing servicing.

Customer: Oh, good.

Woman: But in the unlikely event of any problems, you just send the faulty product back to us and we'll replace it free of charge, no questions asked.

Customer: OK.

Maria: We're running a very big advertising campaign next month in all the major business magazines. So people are going to be looking for the product in the shops.

Customer: All right. I see.

Maria: Now, the best thing about this product is that it works in 5 languages: English, German, French, Spanish and Italian. Just press the F key to change the languages.

Customer: That's good.

Maria: We have large stocks in our warehouse in Austria. We could ship your order within a week.

Customer: All right. Well, I just have one question . . .

Peter: Good morning, Pocket Reader sales and information. My name's Peter. How may I help you?

Customer: Hello, Peter. Um…could you tell me more about the Pocket Reader, please?

Peter: Certainly, how much do you already know about it?

Customer: Well, I've seen your ad in the *Economist*.

Peter: OK, and…er…do you have any questions about the information in the advertisement?

Customer: Yes, yeah. It mentions an interface. What does that mean?

Peter: There's a small cable which plugs into the right side of the Pocket Reader and the other end goes into the serial socket on your computer. The software is on a CD-ROM which comes in the box with the product. You can download text to a PC in just a few seconds.

Customer: Mm, and another question: how big is it?

Peter: Er…the picture in the ad is life size. The length is 16 centimetres. It'll easy fit in a pocket or small handbag. It's remarkably small.

Customer: I see, and…and there seem to be…um…several symbols on the product. What do they mean?

Peter: Well, er…the one on the right is the power on and off switch. And the one on the left with the arrow pointing left is the one you press when you want to . . .

Peter: . . . if you buy this product, you'll be able to read any document wherever you are – on a train, in a library, in a restaurant. There's no need to make notes, or photocopies. You can just read the relevant information into the product.

Customer: Yes, it sounds quite good. But I bet it's not compatible with Macintosh.

Peter: Oh, but it is. You can download the software from our website.

Customer: Really!

Peter: The best thing about this product is that you can take it anywhere and read any document. It's the only

product that will do this.

Customer: Yes, I see. I'm impressed.

Peter: Would you like to place an order?

Customer: Er…just one more question first . . .

Unit 39 B1

Alan: . . . Well, good morning, everyone.

Audience: Morning!

Alan: Good, good. Becky and I are going to tell you about our new…er…advertising campaign. Now, er…ooh, can you hear me all right?

Audience: Yes, all right.

Alan: Oh, good, good. Right, well, first of all let me…let me remind you of last season's advertisements. Er…wh . . . Here's the one we used in April. *[holds up magazine advertisement]* Now, can you see it all right?

Audience: Not very well, no. Not very good actually.

Alan: Oh, right, well in that case…um…probably better if I pass it around…er…and then you can all have a look. Oh, but I'll need to back because it's the only one I've got . . .

Alan: . . . and it all went very well but . . . Sorry, yes, Mrs Wilson?

Mrs Wilson: Did you do any market research to find out consumers' reactions to this?

Alan: Y…well, I . . . I'm not sure about that. Can I…Can I come back to that later, please?

Mrs Wilson: All right.

Alan: Oh, good, right, so to another reason…er…why we thought that…er…we would . . .

Alan: . . . Right, well, I'm afraid I'm out of time now. So there won't be any more time for you to ask me questions. Sorry. Um…I am sorry, I didn't realize it would take this long. Anyway, now I'd like to hand over to Becky. Er…she s going to tell you a…about the new ad and the…er…the thinking behind it.

Becky: Well, thank you, Alan. Yes, I'm going to show you different versions of the ad and explain to you why we chose the one we did choose. But first I want to just outline why we decided a new advertisement was needed. Is that all right?

Audience: Yes, OK, yes.

Becky: OK, right, first of all, we wanted to make sure . . .

Becky: . . . and then, as you can see, now I ve prepared a mock-up of each ad. Now, the first one you can see on the screen . . .

Audience: Haha!

Becky: And it really is silly, I mean, you can . . . I know, the picture really isn't suitable, is it? And that's exactly why we rejected it. Now this one is quite different, look at the detail in . . .

Becky: . . . you can see, I think it works really well. So, thank you very much for listening. And I think you all agree that we've made the right choice. This new ad is really going to improve our profile in the market place. Now, do you have any questions?

Man: Yeah, could you tell us what time . . .

Files

1 You are at an international conference. Role play THREE meetings with people you haven't met before. Talk to each other for a couple of minutes in the break before the next session.

1st meeting	2nd meeting	3rd meeting
Time: 11:00 am	Time: 12:30 pm	Time: 4:30 pm
You are:	You are:	You are:

Begin your conversations like this:

Hello, may I introduce myself, I'm . . .   Hello, my name's . . .

and finish your conversations like this:

Well, it was nice to talk to you.   Yes, maybe see you later.

2 You and your partner work for the same company. You know Ms Stakis, a client, quite well. Answer your partner's questions about her.

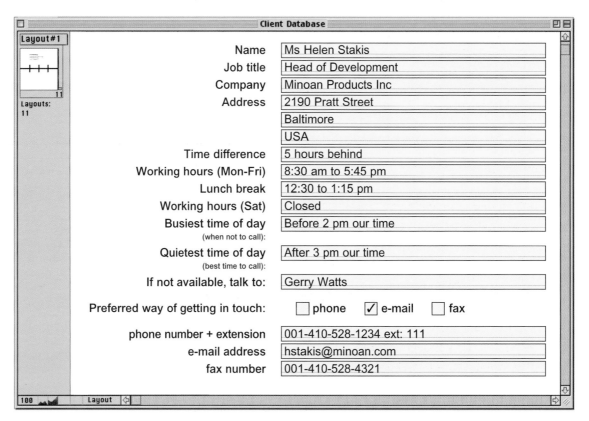

The Client Database shows:

- **Name:** Ms Helen Stakis
- **Job title:** Head of Development
- **Company:** Minoan Products Inc
- **Address:** 2190 Pratt Street / Baltimore / USA
- **Time difference:** 5 hours behind
- **Working hours (Mon–Fri):** 8:30 am to 5:45 pm
- **Lunch break:** 12:30 to 1:15 pm
- **Working hours (Sat):** Closed
- **Busiest time of day (when not to call):** Before 2 pm our time
- **Quietest time of day (best time to call):** After 3 pm our time
- **If not available, talk to:** Gerry Watts
- **Preferred way of getting in touch:** ☐ phone ☑ e-mail ☐ fax
- **phone number + extension:** 001-410-528-1234 ext: 111
- **e-mail address:** hstakis@minoan.com
- **fax number:** 001-410-528-4321

3 You are the new person in the office. Ask your colleague these questions:

> What are the working hours?
>
> Is it OK to call colleagues by their first name?
>
> Should I go round the office introducing myself to everyone?
>
> Is there a dress code in the office? What sort of clothes should I not wear?
>
> Do you have a Dress Down Day? What sort of clothes should I wear that day?
>
> When is lunchtime? How long do we have for lunch?
>
> Who should I talk to if I have a problem?

If there's time, look at your partner's file (File 34) and switch roles.

4 You and your partner are working in the same office. There are eight different mini-situations to role-play.

In the ODD-numbered situations, tell your partner what your problem is – then ask for help, wait to be offered help, or ask if it's OK to take action yourself.

In the EVEN-numbered situations, reply to your partner. Offer to help if you feel like helping.

1 You're very thirsty – you need a drink. Ask your partner to get you a drink.
2 Listen to your partner and then reply to what he or she says.
3 You want to make a private phone call.
4 Reply to what your partner says.
5 You're feeling very hot.
6 Reply to what your partner says.
7 You are feeling unwell – maybe you should go home.
8 Reply to what your partner says.

5 You are head of the Design Team. Study this information before the meeting.

> **Information to give in your report**
>
> Old SPECTRUM Mark 1 design criticized for its 90s style and lack of consumer appeal
>
> New design ready on March 1st – new colours will be blue and red, not grey
>
> Testing begins March 5th after feedback from other teams
>
> **Queries for other teams**
>
> Will 12,000 be enough for the first run?
>
> How will customers feel if there's a delay?

If you are in the chair, look at File 52 for more information.

6 Your partner has the same price list, but you each have different lines of missing information. Fill in the missing information that your partner gives you.

catalogue number	description	price ex VAT	price inc VAT
MON 255B	17-inch flat screen colour monitor	€ 451	€ 529.93
	600 dpi scanner		
FWD 43	Firewire 20 gigabite	€ 140	€ 164.50
	Interface kit		
MMS 9	Superglide mouse mat	€ 12	€ 14.10
	DVD drive		
KB 110	Extended keyboard	€ 124	€ 145.70

7 This role play is in two parts. In part 1 you're making calls, in part 2 you're receiving calls.
Your name is Sam West of Compass International in Manchester.
Your phone number is 44 161 77 66 67, extension 44.

1 The time now is 12:15. Make five SEPARATE calls to these people:

Mr White	– if not available, ask when he's free
Ms Black	– if not available, ask her to call you after lunch
Mr Greene	– if not available, you'll phone him at 4 pm
Mrs Gray	– if not available, find out when she's back in the office
Alex East	– arrange to meet for a drink this evening

2 The time now is 2:15. You'll receive calls for these people in your office. Tell the caller when they'll be back and/or take a message.

APPOINTMENTS

Mr Norton	not at his desk, but certainly in today
Mrs O'Grady	on the other line
Mr Hammond	back at 3 pm
Ms Burns	in a meeting

8 Read this e-mail you have received from the Eldorado Hotel:

We regret to inform you that we have no rooms available for the dates you have requested. As you may know, this is our busiest time of the year and, in common with other hotels in the city, all our rooms are booked for that period.

Are you going to book the expensive accommodation at the Phoenix, or try elsewhere? When you've decided, look at File 60 for more information.

9 This role play is in FOUR parts so that you have two turns at receiving the information.

1 You are Jo Redman, calling Tim Hobbs. Give him this information:

> **Good news:**
> The prices of our products have gone down.
> You ordered 50 boxes of catalogue number RR 1414 at $8.90 per box.
> The price is now $7.90 per box.
> So the total to pay will be £395 not £445.
> Would you like a refund, or a credit on your next order?

2 Janet Henson is away today. You are her assistant. Answer the phone and note down the information you're given. At the end remember to check that you've noted it down correctly.

3 You are Jo Redman, calling Tim Hobbs again. Give him this information:

> **Bad news:**
> Our catalogue number RR 1414 is discontinued from next month.
> We still have inventory to supply up to 500 more boxes, but you must order tomorrow.
> New product: RR 1414A will cost $9.90 per box – new design and more colourful packaging.
> Please let me know if you want to place an order.
> Fax number: 0078 1770 3399

4 Janet Henson is still away. You are her assistant. Answer the phone and note down the information you're given.

10

1 You are Jonathan Weill. Call your partner and leave this message for Terry Williams:

> **Message for Terry Williams from Mr Jonathan Weill**
>
> Please send me 4 catalogues + price lists in US dollars by FedEx or UPS to arrive before Friday:
>
> Mr Jonathan Weill, Skookum Enterprises, 1900 Lakeside Drive, Sheboygan, Wisconsin, USA – zip code: WI 53081
>
> My customers are specially interested in your deluxe range of products.
>
> Call me Monday to talk about the products after I have received the catalogues.
>
> E-mail me today to confirm you have sent the catalogues (jweill@skookum.com).

2 Your partner will call you. Write down the message you're given for Betty Wilson, your colleague. Double-check spellings and numbers.

3 Rewrite your notes so that you can answer *Yes* to all the questions in the Checklist on page 21.

You are Student A. This role play is in THREE parts. **Highlight** the important points in the role information BEFORE you begin the calls.

1 **Call Student B.** Note down the questions you need to ask before you begin. Student C will listen to you both and give feedback after your call. DON'T look at Student B during the call.

> You are Andrea Rossi, calling Hiroshi Miyagi.
> - Confusion about Mr Miyagi's order: your computer is down so you can't check the details.
> - Ask him for the missing information here:
>
> | quantity | colour | catalogue number | shipment date |
> |----------|--------|------------------|---------------|
> | .... boxes of | .... | WS 43 | .... |
> | .... boxes of | .... | WJ 552 | .... |
>
> - You can't ship these before tomorrow.
> - Promise to call back to confirm when the order has been processed.

When you finish, Student C will give you feedback.

2 **Student C will call you.** Student B will listen to you both and give feedback after your call. DON'T look at Student C during the call.

> You are Sandy Anderson. Answer the phone. You met the caller, Jackie Brown, at a trade fair.
> - Agree to meet him/her in your office – agree on a suitable day and time next week.
> - Suggest a tour of your factory.
> - Suggest lunch after the meeting and tour: find out what kind of food he/she likes.
> - Say you'll book a restaurant.
> - Say you'll try to arrange a meeting with your Production Manager.

When you finish, Student B will give you feedback.

3 **Listen to Student B calling Student C.** Use the Checklist on page 23 and rate each person on a scale of 1 to 5: 5 = very good   3 = OK   1 = not very good.

When they finish, give feedback to Students B and C on their call.

 You are a team leader working on a project with your partner, another team leader. You made notes on the schedule but they are incomplete. Telephone your colleague and ask him/her questions to find out the missing information.

Date	Time	Venue	Event	People involved
1 April	13:30–	Boardroom	Planning meeting	AWC + team leaders + one member of each team
14 April	12:00–14:00		Progress reports	Team leaders only
16 April	all day	Branches		All team members
19 April	10:00–12:30	AWC's office	1st progress meeting	
28 April		Boardroom		AWC + team leaders + board members
15 May	07:30–14:00	Main hall		AWC + team leaders + one member of each team

13

1 Find out how your partner got on in the role play:
- How successful was the call?
- What would you do differently if you could do it again?

2 Work together to prepare for this call. Decide more or less what you're going to say before you actually begin the role play.

> You are **Sarah Price**. You promised to call Mr Kelly on Friday but it slipped your mind. When you called on Monday there was no answer. He might be on holiday. Now it's Tuesday, try again.
>
> This is the information he wants about Product code 893:
> Voltage: 110/220 – switches automatically
> Wattage: 25 watts
> Dimensions (height x depth x width): 220 mm x 143 mm x 235 mm
> Colours: blue, green

3 Split up, join a different person and make your call. DON'T look at each other during the call.

4 If there's time, do one or both of the role plays again. See if you can do better this time!

14

Your colleague works in a different branch of your company. Telephone him/her to find out the missing information in this price list.

Catalogue	Make	Model	Description	Our price
CB/45–778G	OLYMPUS	PC111	9 x 21 Compact Porro binoculars	
	PENTAX	UCF Mini	Mini binoculars	£45.53
RT/91–286A		Lunar Cadet 1	F700 Refractor telescope	
	OLYMPUS	PCIIR	10 x 24 Compact binoculars	£59.39
CB/96–184H	MINOLTA		8 x 25 Compact binoculars	
	PENTAX	DFMC	8 x 22 Compact binoculars	£75.23
UB/29–197Y		UCF	10 x 24 UCF binoculars	
	MINOLTA	ACTIVA	10 x 25 Compact binoculars	£59.39
ZB/87–383L	OLYMPUS	PCR	7–15 x 25 Zoom binoculars	
	OLYMPUS	PC11–R	8 x 24 Porro prism binoculars	£60.38
RT/39–129M	HELIOS		F900 Refractor telescope	
	HELIOS	HR	10 x 50 binoculars	£94.04

15

You are sitting with a business associate you don't know very well. Make small talk while you wait for your meeting to begin.

Ask questions to find out what topics your associate is interested in. Ask follow-up questions to keep the conversation going. Show an interest in what your associate says to you.

Try to say as little as possible yourself and encourage your associate to say as much as possible. There should be no awkward silences! Don't talk about business.

1 Work together to prepare for this call. Decide more or less what you're going to say before you actually begin the role play.

> You are **Terry Green**, assistant to Mrs Smith. Yesterday Mr Brown called and you took down a message for Mrs Smith. Last night you must have dropped it in the waste bin.
> Now it's 4 pm – phone Mr Brown and ask him to give you the message again.

2 Split up, join a different person and make your call. DON'T look at each other during the call.

3 Look at File 13 for your next role.

---

17 You and your partner work in the sales department of Corsair Products International. You're looking at your firm's catalogue. Ask each other questions to find out the information you need. The notes in red show information you need to find out. The notes in blue show information you know.

Corsair number	Colours available	List price	Corsair price each 25	50	100
G38–VSF 41	(GY WE RD)	1.95	1.59	1.39	0.99
G39–RJK 21	BK GN BE	4.95	4.90	4.50	3.99
G40–PPP 77	(OE) BF YW	12.95	9.99	8.99	7.99
G41–TPC 83	(PK) WE GY	10.00	9.20	8.30	7.40
G42–UUW 12	WE only	5.20	5.20	5.20	5.20
G43–NNM 77	(SR) GD	20.00	19.00	15.00	10.00

BE = blue   BK = black   GN = green   YW = yellow

G 38 – GY? WE? RD?

G 39 – Blue out of stock. Expected 12 Jan.

G 40 – Now only available in yellow.

G 40 – OE?

G 41 – Total saving on 50?

G 41 – PK??

G 42 – Only 90 in stock. None on order.

G 43 – SR??

G 43 – Total saving on 80?

Your colleague works in a different branch of your firm. You need to meet him/her THREE times next week. Each meeting should last about one hour. The branches are half an hour away from each other – or you could meet midway at a restaurant.

Decide when and where to hold each of the three meetings.

MONDAY
9am	meeting with Bob
11 am	
1 pm	expecting call from Italy
3 pm	meeting with Helen
5 pm	

TUESDAY
9am	
11 am	expecting call from Australia
1 pm	
3 pm	meeting with Jenny
5 pm	

WEDNESDAY
9am	
11 am	Tony
1 pm	meeting with Jeff
3 pm	
5 pm	Golf Club

THURSDAY
9am	meeting with Sharon
11 am	working on report
1 pm	
3 pm	meeting with Lisa
5 pm	

19

You work for the West branch of your company. You're meeting your counterpart from the East branch in your office. You're going to discuss arrangements for a get-together for the staff of the two branches. Look at the Agenda – the questions you want to ask and the information you want to give are in blue.

When your colleague knocks on the door, welcome him/her and offer a seat.

<u>Agenda</u>

<u>Arrangements for 'West meets East' social event</u>

1 Evening or weekend? — West staff prefer Sunday

2 Venue: West Park or East Park? — What is East Park like?

3 Picnic or open-air restaurant? — What do East staff prefer?

4 Invite partners, children and friends? — Partners + children – Yes, but not sure about friends?

5 Limit on numbers? — We have 15 at West branch + families & friends will be about 35

6 Cost: who will pay? — Suggest $5 per head – company will subsidize the main costs

7 Arrangements for bad weather? — Postpone to following Sunday if wet weather forecast

8 Any other business? — We need people to organize games and stuff in the park. Who will do it?

20

You tried to persuade Mr Tucker to go ahead with part or all of the order. Here is his reply.

Arcadia
Hotel and Leisure Group
100 Beach Road EMPYRIA

6th February 20–

Dear Alex,

Thank you for writing to me. After consulting my leisure team we have decided to go ahead with the order. The remaining items can follow when they are ready.

You pointed out that alternative colours are available. We will take them instead of the colours I originally specified.

As the Dinna chairs are no longer available, are you prepared to let us have Snakka chairs for the price of the Dinna chairs?

Best regards,

Don Tucker

Leisure Club Director

21 You are the buyers, King and Co. Read these notes on what you want to achieve. Prioritize your requirements:

✓✓✓ = high priority   ✓✓ = medium priority   ✓ = low priority

You do want to buy the Prima Nova.

It is a good product and ideal for your needs.

2-year warranty	Ask for full warranty with free parts and labour.	....
Shipping	Ask for delivery within 24 hours.	....
Special labelling	Ask for King logo on each unit at no extra charge.	....
Price per unit	Offer to pay $90.	....
Size of order and discount	Offer to place initial order for 40 units now, another 60 in 6 months. Try to get discount of 20% for all 100 units ordered.	....

[Normal discount: 20% for orders over 100 units, 10% for orders over 50 units]

Future orders	Offer to place a regular order every 6 months for two years.	....

22 You are the host. You have spoken to your visitor on the phone, but not met in person before. First, decide if you're going to give a gift to welcome him/her – and if so, what gift?

1 The time is 10:30. Welcome your visitor. He/She is late.
2 He/She is taller than you expected.
3 Find out about your visitor's journey.
4 Offer some coffee.
5 You have organized a tour of the factory for 11 am.
6 Find out if he/she wants to make any phone calls.
7 Show him/her your new catalogue.
8 Offer him/her a gift (if you have decided to do this).

23 Ask your partner questions to find out the missing information in this organizational chart. Use the same kind of questions as the ones in B2 on page 75.

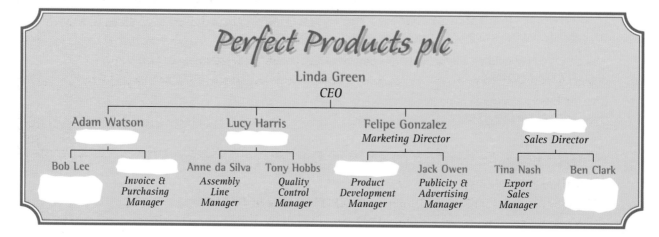

Perfect Products plc

Linda Green
CEO

Adam Watson   Lucy Harris   Felipe Gonzalez   Sales Director
                                          Marketing Director

Bob Lee   Invoice & Purchasing Manager   Anne da Silva   Tony Hobbs   Product Development Manager   Jack Owen   Tina Nash   Ben Clark
                                                        Assembly Line Manager   Quality Control Manager   Publicity & Advertising Manager   Export Sales Manager

24 **You are the guest. You have a free weekend in the city. Ask your host the following questions:**

- What is the population of this city?
- What are the main industries?
- How easy is it to get a ticket for the opera/theatre?
- What do you recommend I should do on Saturday if the weather's nice?
- Where can I go to see the local people having fun?
- Can you recommend a nice walk?
- I feel like getting out of the city on Sunday. Is there somewhere nice I can go by public transport?
  +
- Invite him/her to join you for dinner at your hotel on Sunday evening.

25 **This role play is in TWO parts so that you can play both parts.**

1 You are the receptionist. Refer to this information when answering the guest's questions:

> Allbooks is a good bookstore. It's opposite City Hall.
> Checkout time is 12 noon. There is a baggage room on this floor.
> Dinner: 19:00–22:00
> Lunch: 12:15–13:45
> The maintenance engineer is on duty in 10 minutes.
> The opera house is being rebuilt.
> There is a good symphony concert tonight (seats available $25–$50).

2 You are the business guest. Talk to the receptionist about the following:

- Ask the receptionist to recommend a nice place to eat.
- Find out when breakfast is served.
- Find out why the lift isn't working.
- You want to go to the airport. Is it best to take a taxi or public transport?
- You want to reserve a table for 4 people for dinner tomorrow.
- You think the hotel has charged you too much for phone calls.

26 **Read this e-mail you have received from the Phoenix Hotel:**

The only rooms we have available for the days you require are the Penthouse Suite with two adjoining rooms and lounge area. As a special favour to you, we can offer the Suite for a special price of $500 per night.

Decide if you will take these rooms.

If *Yes*, write an e-mail to the Phoenix Hotel. Then look at File 60.

If *No*, write an e-mail to the Eldorado Hotel. Then look at File 8.

27 Study these instructions. Then, in your own words, explain to your partner how to change an inkjet cartridge.

1

Press the Power button ⓪ to turn on the printer.
Release the button when the Power light ⓪ is on.

2

Open the access door. Press the Change Print Cartridge button ⑪ to move the print cartridge cradle to the loading position.

The Change Print Cartridge light ⑪ will blink.

Remove the old cartridge.

3

Take the new black print cartridge and remove the tape(s) covering the ink nozzles. Be careful not to touch the ink nozzles and the copper ribbon.

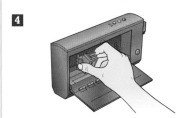

4

Place the print cartridge into the cradle, with the arrow on the cartridge top pointing toward the printer.

Be careful not to slide the print cartridge against the back of the cradle. A sliding motion could damage the electrical contacts on the print cartridge cradle.

5

Push the top of the print cartridge forward, snapping it into place.

6

Press the Change Print Cartridge button ⑪.

The print cartridge cradle returns to the "home" position and the Change Print Cartridge light ⑪ goes off.

Close the access door.

28 Study this description of how a pocket calculator works. Then ask your partner questions to find out the missing information.

You want to add 5 and 4, so . . .

You press the ⑤ key on keypad (Input Unit) ▸ code stored as 0101 in _____ Unit

You press the PLUS key ▸ code stored as 1101 – this is the _____ code

You press the ④ key ▸ code stored as 0100

You press the EQUALS key ▸ Signal sent to _____ Unit

Processor Unit takes the operation code and stored numbers and performs the operation (adding the numbers)

Result 1001 sent to _____

Decoder changes the 4-bit binary result into 7-bit binary code

Result _____ sent to Output Unit (Liquid Crystal Display)

Electric pulse of 1 bit creates a _____ segment on LCD
(0 is no electrical pulse and segment remains light)

Result appears on LCD as 9

Input unit ▸ Microchip (contains Memory Unit, Processor Unit, Decoder) ▸ Output Unit

29

Imagine that you work for a wholesaler and it's your job to interest retailers in this product.
You're going to have to tell your customer about this product soon. Here are some questions the customer may ask. How can you answer them?

- What are the product's features?
- Why should I buy it?
- Why will my customers want to buy it from me?
- What is special about the product?

Lingo 10 Talk

language translator

The Lingo 10 Talk is the first language translator that translates into foreign language characters and shows you phonetically how to pronounce the characters in your own language, and then pronounces them for you!

The Lingo 10 Talk translates English, German, French, Spanish, Italian, Portuguese, Russian, Chinese, Japanese and Korean.

- Translates over 80,000 Words
- 5,000 Useful and Popular Phrases
- Clear Sound Quality
- 32K Databank for storing appointments, addresses and phone numbers
- 4 Line x 16 Character LCD Display

- 8 Currency Conversions
- 6 Metric Conversions
- 10 Digit Talking Calculator
- Local Time 12/24 Hour Format
- World Time in 200 Cities
- Alarm Feature

Suggested retail price: $100

 30

This is a model e-mail for A3 on page 28.

Inbox ⬛⬜✖

| From: | Sam Morton <smorton@foresight.co.uk> | To: | Fritz Knaup <fknaup@durchsicht.de> |
| Subject: | Visit to Germany | Date: | Thu, 25 Nov 20– 00:13:22 +0100 |

Dear Fritz,

My flight on Friday has been rescheduled. New arrival time is 8:45, not 10:30.
Please DON'T meet me at the airport – I'll get a taxi to your office, arriving by about 10:00.

We'll have time to talk about the project before we go to meet Mrs Neumann at 11:30.

Can you book a table at the Golden Gate Restaurant for the three of us for 1 o'clock?
By the way, don't forget to tell them she's a vegetarian.

See you on Friday. If there are any delays, I'll call you at the office.

Any problems, call me on my cell phone: 0789 923 81945.

Best wishes,

Sam

31 You are at an international conference. Role play THREE meetings with people you haven't met before. Talk to each other for a couple of minutes in the break before the next session.

1st meeting	2nd meeting	3rd meeting
Time: 11:00 am	Time: 12:30 pm	Time: 4:30 pm
You are:	You are:	You are:

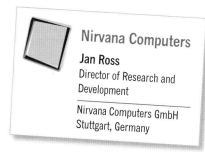

ROCKHARD MOUNTAIN BIKES Inc
Jo Chan
Purchasing Director
San Francisco, California
USA

Nirvana Computers
Jan Ross
Director of Research and Development
Nirvana Computers GmbH
Stuttgart, Germany

Worldwide Travel Agency
Pat Miller
Business Travel Director
Worldwide Travel Agency Ltd
Birmingham, UK

Begin your conversations like this:

Hello, may I introduce myself, I'm . . .   Hello, my name's . . .

and finish your conversations like this:

Well, it was nice to talk to you.   Yes, maybe see you later.

32 You and your partner work for the same company. You know Mr Suzuki, a client, quite well. Answer your partner's questions about him.

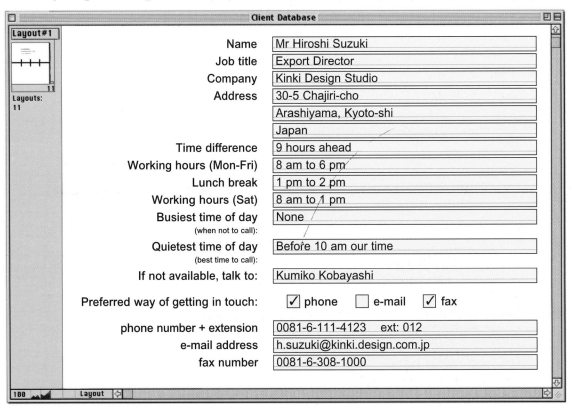

	Client Database
Name	Mr Hiroshi Suzuki
Job title	Export Director
Company	Kinki Design Studio
Address	30-5 Chajiri-cho
	Arashiyama, Kyoto-shi
	Japan
Time difference	9 hours ahead
Working hours (Mon-Fri)	8 am to 6 pm
Lunch break	1 pm to 2 pm
Working hours (Sat)	8 am to 1 pm
Busiest time of day (when not to call):	None
Quietest time of day (best time to call):	Before 10 am our time
If not available, talk to:	Kumiko Kobayashi
Preferred way of getting in touch:	☑ phone ☐ e-mail ☑ fax
phone number + extension	0081-6-111-4123 ext: 012
e-mail address	h.suzuki@kinki.design.com.jp
fax number	0081-6-308-1000

33 If you tried to persuade Mr Tucker to go ahead with part or all of the order, look at File 20. If you regretfully accepted his decision, look at File 51.

34 You are the local person in the office. Answer your new colleague's questions. Try to be friendly by asking some of these questions to make him or her feel welcome.

> Are there any questions you'd like to ask me?
>
> Is this your first visit to this country?
>
> What do you think of this country?
>
> Where are you living?
>
> How long are you staying here?
>
> Do you like our food?
>
> Would you like to join me for lunch?
>
> Would you like to join me for a drink after work?

If there's time, look at your partner's file (File 3) and switch roles.

35 You and your partner are working in the same office. There are eight different mini-situations to role-play.

In the EVEN-numbered situations, tell your partner what your problem is – then ask for help, wait to be offered help, or ask if it's OK to take action yourself.

In the ODD-numbered situations, reply to your partner. Offer to help if you feel like helping.

1 Listen to your partner and then reply to what he or she says.
2 You want to use your partner's computer. Ask your partner's permission.
3 Reply to what your partner says.
4 You're very hungry – your partner has some sandwiches.
5 Reply to what your partner says.
6 You have to make an important phone call.
7 Reply to what your partner says.
8 You want to go to the toilet/bathroom.

36 You are head of the Production Team. Study this information before the meeting.

> **Information to give in your report**
> First production run scheduled for March 20th – first run will be 12,000 units
> Ready for packing on 24th and due in warehouse on April 1st
> Second production run scheduled for May 1st – second run will be 5,000 units
>
> **Queries for other teams**
> How long will feedback take?
> Will 5,000 be enough for the second run?

If you are in the chair, look at File 52 for more information.

37 Your partner has the same price list, but you each have different lines of missing information. Fill in the missing information that your partner gives you.

catalogue number	description	price ex VAT	price inc VAT
MON 255B	17-inch flat screen colour monitor	€ 451	€ 529.93
USB 129	600 dpi scanner	€ 99	€ 116.33
	Firewire 20 gigabite		
IF430	Interface kit	€ 49	€ 57.58
	Superglide mouse mat		
DVD 191	DVD drive	€ 101	€ 118.68
	Extended keyboard		

38 This role play is in two parts. In part 1 you're receiving calls, in part 2 you're making calls.
Your name is Alex East of Orbit International in Birmingham.
Your phone number is 44 121 88 94 47, extension 981.

1 The time now is 12:15. You'll receive calls for these people in your office. Tell the caller when they'll be back and/or take a message.

> APPOINTMENTS
> Mr White   lunch 12–1
> Ms Black   meeting a client
> Mr Greene   out of the office this morning
> Mrs Gray   on holiday this week

2 The time now is 2:15. Make five SEPARATE calls to these people:

Mr Norton   – if not available, ask when he's free
Ms O'Grady   – if not available, ask her to phone you before 3 pm
Mr Hammond   – if not available, you'll phone him at 4 pm
Ms Burns   – if not available, ask her to call you urgently
Sam West   – arrange to have lunch next week

39 You are head of the Sales Team. Study this information before the meeting.

> **Information to give in your report**
> Customers waiting for new SPECTRUM Mark 2 – a lot of interest
> Definite pre-orders of 5,000 already + 5,000 will probably be ordered in March
> Catalogue says Mark 2 will be available 'at the end of March'
>
> **Queries for other teams**
> What if major changes have to be made after feedback?
> Will the units definitely be in the warehouse on April 1st?

If you are in the chair, look at **File 52** for more information.

40 This role play is in FOUR parts so that you have two turns at receiving the information.

1 Tim Hobbs is away today. You are his assistant. Answer the phone and note down the information you're given. At the end remember to check that you've noted it down correctly.

2 Now you are Pat Scott, calling Janet Henson. Give her this information:

Good news:
Rainbow Products in Hong Kong have become our sole supplier.
They can now offer you 20% discount on all orders over $US 500.
To qualify you must quote this reference number: JG 2000
and place orders by e-mail.
Their e-mail address: sales@rainbow.com.hk

3 Tim Hobbs is still away. You are his assistant. Answer the phone and note down the information you're given.

4 You are Pat Scott, calling Janet Henson again. Give her this information:

Bad news:
Rainbow Products have gone out of business.
All money paid to them is lost.
If you have paid them anything let me know immediately.
We will refund any payment under $US 900.
My e-mail is: pscott@jeopardy.products.com

41 1 You are Dan Crockett. Your partner will call you. Write down the message you're given for Terry Williams, your colleague. Double-check spellings and numbers.

2 Call your partner and leave this message for Betty Wilson:

Message for Betty Wilson from Dan Crockett

We have closed our premises in Melbourne due to storm damage. We have opened a new warehouse in Gold Coast, Queensland.

Please don't ship our order to Melbourne. Instead please ship to Gold Coast: Dan Crockett, Bonzer Products, 1910 Ocean Drive, Surfers Paradise, Queensland, Australia 4217

Please also note new phone and fax numbers:
phone: 0061 7 893 1238
fax: 0061 7 982 1895

E-mail or fax me today to confirm that you have got this message and that the shipment will not go to Melbourne: dancrockett@bonzer.com.au

3 Rewrite your notes so that you can answer *Yes* to all the questions in the Checklist on page 21.

You are Student B. This role play is in THREE parts. **Highlight the important points in the role information BEFORE you begin the calls.**

1 Student A will call you. Student C will listen to you both and give feedback after your call. DON'T look at Student A during the call.

> You are Hiroshi Miyagi. Answer the phone. You are expecting this shipment from Mr Rossi:
>
> | quantity | colour | catalogue number | shipment date |
> |---|---|---|---|
> | 50 boxes of | green | WJ 552 | yesterday |
> | 25 boxes of | blue | WS 43 | yesterday |
>
> • The order is urgent and shipment was promised for yesterday.
> • You need the goods by next Wednesday at the latest – ask him to tell you when the order has been processed.

When you finish, Student C will give you feedback.

2 Listen to Student C calling Student A. Use the Checklist on page 23 and rate each person on a scale of 1 to 5: 5 = very good   3 = OK   1 = not very good.

When they finish, give feedback to Students A and C on their call.

3 Call Student C. Note down the questions you need to ask before you begin. Student A will listen to you both and give feedback after your call. DON'T look at Student C during the call.

> You are Sean O'Neill, calling Terry Chandler. You work in different branches of the same firm.
> • You are going to the Montex conference next month. Ask if Mr/Ms Chandler is going too.
> • You are driving, and he/she could come in your car. By car it takes 4 hours.
> • You can get 50% discount at the Seaview Hotel – friendly small hotel on the seafront. Offer to book a room for him/her.
> • You plan to return on the Sunday afternoon, leaving at lunchtime.
> • Find out when he/she is giving a presentation.

When you finish, Student A will give you feedback.

 You are a team leader working on a project with your partner, another team leader. You made notes on the schedule but they are incomplete. Call your colleague and ask him/her questions to find out the missing information.

Date	Time	Venue	Event	People involved
1 April	13:30–16:45		Planning meeting	AWC + team leaders + one member of each team
14 April	–14:00	Canteen	Progress reports	
16 April		Branches	Team meetings	All team members
19 April	–12:30		1st progress meeting	AWC + team leaders
28 April	18:30–21:00	Boardroom	2nd progress meeting	
15 May		Main hall	Final presentations	AWC + team leaders + one member of each team

44 **1** Find out how your partner got on in the role play:

- How successful was the call?
- What would you do differently if you could do it again?

2 Work together to prepare for this call. Decide more or less what you're going to say before you actually begin the role play.

> You are **Tim Kelly**. Sarah Price promised to call you on Friday but she didn't. Now it's Tuesday and still no word from her.
>
> You need information about Product code 893:
> Voltage: ??
> Wattage: ??
> Dimensions: ??
> Available colours: ??
>
> Answer the phone when it rings . . .

3 Split up, join a different person and make your call. DON'T look at each other during the call.

4 If there's time, do one or both of the role plays again. See if you can do better this time!

45 **1** Here are the meanings of the abbreviations on page 20:
February • Friday • Square • Road • Avenue • if possible • information
as soon as possible • number • For your information • By the way • inclusive/including
Please turn over (turn the page) • Re: = concerning/regarding

2 And here are some more useful abbreviations:

$10m	= ten million dollars	Inc	= incorporated
@	= at	Ltd	= limited (company)
CEO	= chief executive officer	p & p	= postage and packing
cc	= 'carbon copy' (copy to . . .)	pa	= per annum (per year)
bcc	= 'blind carbon copy' (copy to someone when you don't want them to know who else has got a copy)	PA	= personal assistant
		plc	= public limited company
		pp (per pro)	= signed on behalf of
c/o	= care of	St	= Street OR Saint
enc	= enclosure	VAT	= value added tax
ext	= extension number	& Co	= and Company

46 You are sitting with a business associate you don't know very well. Make small talk while you wait for your meeting to begin.

Ask questions to find out what topics your associate is interested in. Ask follow-up questions to keep the conversation going. Show an interest in what your associate says to you.

Encourage your associate to say as much as possible and try to say as little as possible yourself. There should be no awkward silences! Don't talk about business.

47 1 Work together to prepare for this call. Decide more or less what you're going to say before you actually begin the role play.

> You are **George Brown**. Yesterday you left a message for Mrs Smith, asking her to contact you by lunchtime today and to send you three copies of the draft contract.
> It's now 4 pm and she hasn't been in touch. Answer the phone when it rings . . .

2 Split up, join a different person and make your call. DON'T look at each other during the call.

3 Look at File 44 for your next role.

48 You and your partner work in the sales department of Corsair Products International. You're looking at your firm's catalogue. Ask each other questions to find out the information you need. The notes in red show information you need to find out. The notes in blue show information you know.

Corsair number	Colours available	List price	Corsair price each		
			25	50	100
G38–VSF 41	GY WE RD	1.95	1.59	1.39	0.99
G39–RJK 21	BK GN BE	4.95	4.90	4.50	3.99
G40–PPP 77	OE BF YW	12.95	9.99	8.99	7.99
G41–TPC 83	PK WE GY	10.00	9.20	8.30	7.40
G42–UUW 12	WE only	5.20	5.20	5.20	5.20
G43–NNM 77	SR GD	20.00	19.00	15.00	10.00

GY = grey   PK= pink   RD = red   WE = white

G 38 – All colours available. Ample stocks.

G 39 – BK? GN? BE?

G 39 – Total saving on 30?

G 40 – BF??

G 40 – Total saving on 100?

G 41 – Pink no longer available.

G 42 – Total saving on 70?

G 43 – GD??

G 43 – Discontinued.

49 Your colleague works in a different branch of your firm. You need to meet him/her THREE times next week. Each meeting should last about one hour. The branches are half an hour away from each other – or you could meet midway at a restaurant.

Decide when and where to hold each of the three meetings.

MONDAY
9am   Mr Brown
11 am   meeting with Donna
1 pm
3 pm   expecting call from Mexico
5 pm

TUESDAY
9am   meeting with Ken
11 am
1 pm   expecting call from Madrid
3 pm
5 pm   meeting with Joe

WEDNESDAY
9am   Ms Taylor
11 am
1 pm   meeting with Karen
3 pm
5 pm   Golf Club

THURSDAY
9am   meeting with Debbie
11 am
1 pm
3 pm   Susan
5 pm

50 Your colleague works in a different branch of your company. Telephone him/her to find out the missing information in this price list.

Catalogue	Make	Model	Description	Our price
CB/45–778G	OLYMPUS		9 x 21 Compact Porro binoculars	£29.69
MB/89–231J		UCF Mini	10 x 21 Mini binoculars	
	HELIOS	Lunar Cadet 1	F700 Refractor telescope	£48.50
CB/83–289R	OLYMPUS	PCIIR	Compact binoculars	
	MINOLTA	ACTIVA	8 x 25 Compact binoculars	£53.45
CB/29–848B	PENTAX	DFMC	Compact binoculars	
	PENTAX	UCF	10 x 24 UCF binoculars	£66.32
CB/96–186W		ACTIVA	10 x 25 Compact binoculars	
	OLYMPUS	PCR	7–15 x 25 Zoom binoculars	£60.38
PB/95–900N	OLYMPUS	PC11–R	8 x 24 Porro prism binoculars	
	HELIOS	Lunar Cadet 2	F900 Refractor telescope	£83.15
PB/21–667K		HR	10 x 50 binoculars	

 51 You wrote to Mr Tucker about his decision to cancel his order. Here is his reply.

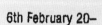

Arcadia
Hotel and Leisure Group
100 Beach Road EMPYRIA

6th February 20–

Dear Alex,

Thank you for writing to me.

I talked to my leisure team about substituting Gypsy chairs and tables for Portico products yesterday. They inform me that the quality of their furniture is very poor. An average chair will last only one season, whereas your products last for two or three.

So I am happy to say that we have decided to go ahead with our order after all. Please supply the unavailable items (in the colours I specified) when they become available.

As the Dinna chairs are no longer available, are you prepared to let us have Snakka chairs for the price of the Dinna chairs?

I seem to remember that there is a discount for orders over €5,000. Is this right?

Best regards,

Don Tucker

Leisure Club Director

52 You are going to chair the meeting. Look at the useful phrases on page 55 before you begin.

1 Welcome everyone and open the meeting.

2 Make sure each member has a chance to speak. Make sure all the points on the agenda are covered in the time available.

3 Thank everyone for their contributions. Close the meeting.

53 You work for the East branch of your company. You're meeting your counterpart from the West branch in his/her office. You're going to discuss arrangements for a get-together for the staff of the two branches. Look at the Agenda — the questions you want to ask and the information you want to give are in blue.

When you're ready, knock on the door. Ask for some coffee before you start.

Agenda

Arrangements for 'West meets East' social event

1	Evening or weekend?	What do West staff prefer?
2	Venue: West Park or East Park?	East Park bigger than West Park, more grassy areas for games and sitting
3	Picnic or open-air restaurant?	East staff prefer picnic — no suitable restaurants in East Park anyway
4	Invite partners, children and friends?	Only staff with no partner can bring two friends max.
5	Limit on numbers?	We have 12 at East Branch + families equals about 40
6	Cost: who will pay?	$5 for each adult. Children free.
7	Arrangements for bad weather?	Set up "hot line" on Saturday to give latest info to everyone. Also info on website?
8	Any other business?	No

---

54 Check your answers. Then change ONE digit in each number. Say the new number aloud to your partner and ask him/her to write the new number down.

1 Phone number: 01 181 776 9672
2 Fax number: 44 1398 134561
3 Reference number: 049 PR 109423 9901 12
4 Bank account number: 52213114
5 Credit card number: 4550 1903 1258 5668
6 Invoice number: PJ 99019
7 Part number: 797M1061011
8 Customer number: WV 028912

55 You are the salespeople, Prima Products. Read these notes on what you want to achieve. Prioritize your requirements:

✓✓✓ = high priority ✓✓ = medium priority ✓ = low priority

You do want to sell the Prima Nova to King and Co.

You want them to place a regular order.

2-year warranty	Offer full warranty with parts and labour at $5 per unit.	....
	Offer warranty with free parts (but not labour).	....
Shipping	Offer delivery in 3 working days.	....
Special labelling	Offer to print King logo on each unit for an extra $2.	....
Price per unit	Ask for $110.	....
Size of order and discount	If they order 40 units now + another 60 in 6 months, offer 10% discount for both orders.	....
[Normal discount: 20% for orders over 100 units, 10% for orders over 50 units]		
Future orders	Offer 20% discount if they place a regular order once a month for two years.	....

56 You are the visitor. You have spoken to your host on the phone, but not met in person before. First, decide what gift you're going to give him/her.

1 The time is 10:30. You are late. Your taxi was hit by a bus. No one was hurt.
2 You have a suitcase. Could someone take it to your hotel?
3 You need to make sure the hotel is expecting you tonight.
4 You are thirsty and want a cold drink.
5 You want to visit the warehouse as well as the factory.
6 You want to check your e-mails. Where can you connect your laptop?
7 Offer him/her the gift you have brought.

57 Ask your partner questions to find out the missing information in this organizational chart. Use the same kind of questions as the ones in B2 on page 75.

58 You are the host. Your guest has a free weekend in the city. Answer the questions he/she asks you, and also:

- Apologize that you can't look after him/her during the weekend. Your aunt and uncle are coming to stay.
- Tell him/her something about the history of the city.
- Recommend a nice restaurant for lunch on Saturday.
- Recommend a good place for shopping.
- Recommend an interesting historic building to visit.
- Recommend a nice place to go on Sunday to get out of the city.
- Invite him/her to visit your home on Sunday evening for dinner.

59 This role play is in TWO parts so that you can play both parts.

1 You are the business guest. Talk to the receptionist about the following:

- Tell the receptionist that the phone in your room doesn't work.
- Find out how much a good seat for the opera costs.
- Ask the receptionist to recommend a good bookstore.
- Find out when lunch is served.
- Find out when dinner is served.
- Find out if you can leave your suitcase in your room till 6 pm.

2 You are the receptionist. Refer to this information when answering the guest's questions:

> A taxi to the airport costs $25, the train is $5. Traffic to the airport can be very slow.
> Breakfast: Mon-Fri 06:00–10:00   Sat–Sun 08:00–10:30
> The elevator is being serviced. It will be working again in 30 minutes.
> The hotel charges $2 per unit for phone calls.
> The hotel restaurant is closed tomorrow.
> The hotel's own restaurant is good value and has very good international cuisine.

60 Read this e-mail you have received from the Phoenix Hotel:

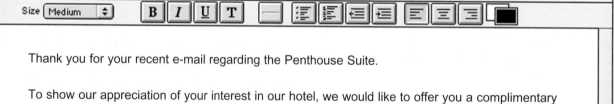

Thank you for your recent e-mail regarding the Penthouse Suite.

To show our appreciation of your interest in our hotel, we would like to offer you a complimentary meal for three people in our Rooftop Restaurant. Please quote reference PH 101 when booking.

Write an e-mail to Ms Rossi, telling her you've booked her accommodation.

61 Study these instructions. Then, in your own words, explain to your partner how to change a laser printer cartridge.

Installing or changing a toner cartridge

Toner is the powdered ink that produces the image on the paper. Follow these steps to install a toner cartridge into the printer.

1. Open the printer access door.

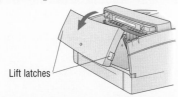

Lift latches

2. If you are replacing a used cartridge, remove the old cartridge and set it aside.

3. Unpack the new toner cartridge and gently rock it to distribute the toner inside.

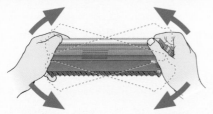

Gently rock the cartridge in a see-saw motion.

4. Pull the tape tab to remove the tape.

Pull the tape completely out.

5. Insert the cartridge into the printer.

Line up the markings on the sides of the cartridge with the arrows in the printer.

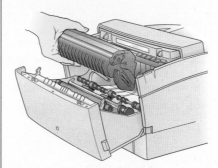

Line up the arrows on the toner cartridge with the arrows inside the printer.

6. Close the access door.

---

62 Study this description of how a pocket calculator works. Then ask your partner questions to find out the missing information.

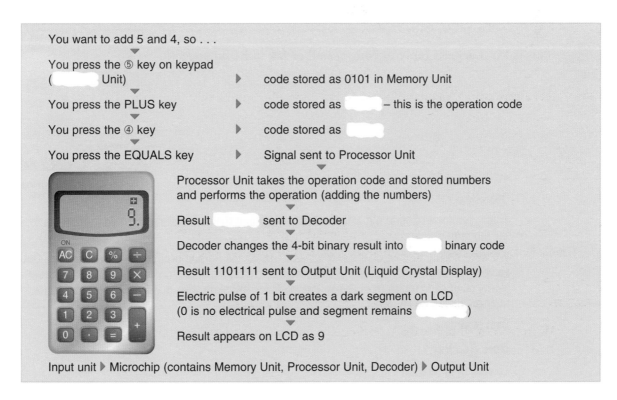

63

You are Student C. This role play is in THREE parts. Highlight the important points in the role information BEFORE you begin the calls.

1 Listen to Student A calling Student B. Use the Checklist on page 23 and rate each person on a scale of 1 to 5:   5 = very good   3 = OK   1 = not very good.
When they finish, give feedback to Students A and B on their call.

2 Call Student A. Note down the questions you need to ask before you begin. Student B will listen to you both and give feedback after your call. DON'T look at Student A during the call.

> You are Jackie Brown, calling Sandy Anderson. You met each other at a trade fair in Hamburg last month.
> - Arrange a visit to Mr/Ms Anderson next week.
> - Agree on a suitable day and time — preferably morning.
> - Lunch would be nice — you don't mind what kind of food. He/She can choose.
> - Ask if he can arrange a meeting with the Production Manager after lunch.
> - Promise to confirm this in writing.

When you finish, Student B will give you feedback.

3 Student B will call you. Student A will listen to you both and give feedback after your call. DON'T look at Student B during the call.

> You are Terry Chandler. Answer the phone. You and Sean O'Neill work in different branches of the same firm.
> - You always go to the Montex conference.
> - You usually go by train (journey time 3 hours), but car would be nice.
> - Your presentation is on Sunday afternoon at 4:30.
> - Say you'll return by train on Sunday evening OR persuade Mr/Ms O'Neill to drive back later.

When you finish, Student A will give you feedback.

64

This is Mr Tucker's reply to your e-mail or fax in B1 on page 49.

Arcadia
Hotel and Leisure Group
100 Beach Road EMPYRIA

4th February 20–

Dear Alex,

Thank you for writing to me with the bad news about the non-availability of your products for the summer season.

We were hoping to have chairs and tables to match the Portico products we already have. But as you cannot supply what we require I wish to cancel the whole order. I now intend to order all my chairs and tables from Gypsy International. Although their quality is lower than yours, their prices are much lower.

Best regards,

Don Tucker

Leisure Club Director

65 These are model e-mails for B1 on page 29.

YOUR ORDER # 111

Dear Mr Adams,
Thank you for your e-mail.
I am sorry to hear that you have not received your order.
The reason is that we can only guarantee Next Day Shipping for orders placed before noon on Friday.
Your order was placed at 4:15 pm and was not shipped until Monday.
You can expect your delivery to arrive today, Tuesday, before 5 pm.
If, for any reason, it does not arrive, please let me know.
Thank you for ordering from us.
Regards,

OUR ORDER # 222

Dear Ms Baker,
Thank you for your e-mail about the delay in shipping this order.
I am sorry to inform you that we have to cancel this order because of the delay.
Our customer wanted the goods by this week at the latest. He has told us that he can't wait any longer.
I hope that we will be able to place another order before too long.
Sincerely,

YOUR ORDER # 333

Dear Mr Collins,
Thank you for your e-mail regarding your order.
I am sorry that only one of the two boxes arrived. I can confirm that both boxes were shipped together.
Could you please let me know the number on the box that did arrive, so that I can check the routing of the missing box.
If the missing box doesn't reach you, or if it is damaged when it comes, we will replace it free of charge.
I will e-mail you tomorrow when I have found out more from the shippers.
Please let me know if the missing box arrives in the meantime.
Yours truly,

---

66 This is a rewritten version of the enthusiastic letter in B1 on page 31.

Dear Mr Black,

I have some good news for you.

To commemorate the relaunch of our TipTop products we are making a special offer for all our regular customers:

The whole range is now available at a special price.

From now until November 30th you can save 25 per cent on all orders from our TipTop range.

I suggest that you place an order this month to take advantage of this special offer.

Looking forward to hearing from you,

Yours truly,

67 This is a model reply from Mr Brown for B3 on page 27

Dear Ms Clark,

Thank you for your fax regarding the problems with our order number 4567.

I am pleased to inform you that shortly after I received your fax, the consignment of goods arrived at our warehouse in good condition.

Apparently, the driver had unloaded the boxes when making a delivery at Johnson's Ltd, and left them there in error. It wasn't till after the weekend that the mistake was discovered and Johnson's very kindly loaded the boxes onto one of their trucks and brought them to our warehouse.

Fortunately, this time the delay did not cause us too much inconvenience. However, we depend on goods arriving on time and we will not place further orders unless you decide to use a more reliable company for future shipments to us.

I hope to hear your decision by the end of the month.

If you have any further questions or would like to discuss this matter, please call me.

Yours sincerely,

David Brown

68 Imagine that you work for a wholesaler and it's your job to interest retailers in this product.
You're going to have to tell your customer about this product soon. Here are some questions the customer may ask. How can you answer them?

- What are the product's features?
- Why should I buy it?
- Why will my customers want to buy it from me?
- What is special about the product?

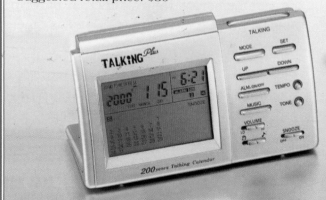

200-YEAR TALKING CALENDAR CLOCK

- A human voice tells you the time and the temperature
- Large, easy-read displays of monthly calendar, year, month, date, day and time
- 1 daily and 3 calendar alarms
- Alarm with 12-minute snooze
- Alarm can be rooster's crow or music
- Temperature in °F or °C
- 15 selections of world-famous music
- Volume control

Suggested retail price: $50